Creating a Positive PUBLIC SCHOOL Experience

ERIC BUEHRER

Publishers Since 1798

THOMAS NELSON PUBLISHERS
Nashville • Atlanta • London • Vancouver

*For Kaitlyn Nicole, who
played quietly at my feet while
I wrote this book. If angels
had bodies then you would
have wings.*

Copyright © 1994 by Eric Buehrer

Published in Nashville, Tennessee, by Thomas Nelson, Inc., Publishers, and distributed in Canada by Word Communications, Ltd., Richmond, British Columbia, and in the United Kingdom by Word (UK), Ltd., Milton Keynes, England.

Unless otherwise noted, Scripture quotations are from THE NEW AMERICAN STANDARD BIBLE, Copyright © 1960, 1962, 1963, 1968, 1971, 1972, 1973, 1975, 1977 by The Lockman Foundation and are used by permission.

Library of Congress Cataloging-in-Publication Data

Buehrer, Eric.
  Creating a positive public school experience / Eric Buehrer.
    p. cm.
  Includes bibliographical references and index.
  ISBN 0–7852–8156–8 (pb)
    1. Education—Parent participation—United States. 2. Public schools—United States. 3. Parent-teacher relationships—United States. I. Title.
LC225.3.B766   1994   94–22029
371′.01—dc20   CIP

Printed in the United States of America
1 2 3 4 5 6 7 — 99 98 97 96 95 94

Contents

1
Take Charge

We all know public schools need reform, but some changes may take years to implement. The immediate issue for you is how to help your child when he goes to school tomorrow. This book will show you exactly what to do to create a positive public school experience!

During the 1980s and continuing into the 1990s, parents have become increasingly aware of the shortcomings of public schools. Headlines and news reports regularly suggest that if your children are in public school they probably aren't getting a good education, their morals may be corrupted, and they may end up feeling cynical about America and maybe even doubting the existence of God.

If you are concerned about your children's education, this book is for you. My message is this: Your children can go to public schools *and* get a good education.

This book will not eliminate your concerns by simply saying that all the troubling stories about public schools are false. Many public schools have serious problems. Some schools do not provide solid academic training. Some do not provide sound moral training. Some teachers may even unwittingly undermine a child's spiritual foundation. Anxiety is not removed by denial. This book provides solutions. It will help you find the good things your child's school is doing and how to capitalize on them. It will also give you practical ways to overcome problems you may encounter with your child's education.

Each chapter of this book will give you knowledge and techniques for maximizing your child's education. The tools come from the seminars I present for public school parents. As a former high school teacher, and now the president of Gateways To Better Education—a ministry dedicated to helping public school parents—I have had the privilege of traveling across America conducting these seminars for parents and hearing the concerns they have regarding their public school. I spend a lot of time on the phone counseling parents about specific situations in their schools. Having spent my career both inside and outside the school system, I have crafted the ten Parent Power Tools detailed in this book. I have seen these principles work for many parents, and I know they can work for you too!

At Gateways to Better Education, our approach is to help parents become "relational activists." We have found that for the last twenty years public school involvement for Christians has been defined almost exclusively as political involvement. Whereas political activity is certainly needed, we see the need to help parents who want to be active in their children's education without necessarily being activists. Our mission is to help you gain greater assurance that your children will become academically accomplished, morally sound, and spiritually strong. We do that by helping you build better relationships with your children and their teachers.

Building relationships requires active participation—that is the key. But any form of education for your children requires some form of action. Parents who homeschool spend from $200 to $1,000 more per year on materials than do most parents of public school children, and they devote between fifteen and thirty hours each week to preparing lessons and tutoring. That is a tremendous time commitment. On the other hand, parents who enroll their children in private schools spend even more money and often volunteer at their child's school. This option requires a substantial financial commitment.

There is a common misperception that while homeschooling takes considerable time and private education takes considerable money, public schooling requires very little of either since it is provided by the state. However, just the opposite is true. Because public education is provided by the state, you should spend a great deal of time monitoring your child's learning and invest money in tools to help your child succeed.

A child's education formulates how he views the world and himself, what he learns to value in life, what kind of character he has, how his spiritual life fits with his physical life, his political views, and his skills for making a living. Education is the act of civilizing the untamed heart and training the unskilled mind. It is moving a child from no knowledge of the arts, sciences, religion, politics, social manners, and other cultural factors to an appreciation of and skill in those areas. Education is a process of refinement. With that in mind, we must acknowledge the complex social and political influences on what is taught in public education.

Political Rather Than Educational

The state is interested primarily in creating a competent work force and peaceful social order. You may have similar goals for your child's education, but your goals reflect your own complex, value-laden set of assumptions. You want to see your child contribute to a peaceful social order, but you may see this arising from a set of moral values that many public school educators do not agree with. You want your child to graduate with competence in a variety of skills. But even on this subject there is wide disagreement among educators over what "competence" is. Although this book is not about how to get involved politically in your school district, you do need to be aware of the political climate of your child's school.

Public schools by their very nature are heavily influenced by politics. Elected school board members sway with the pressures of the electorate, special interest groups, and teachers' unions. State curriculum committees are influenced by the competing agendas of pressure groups at the state capitol. Often school policy and curricula are set for what can best be described as political rather than educational reasons.

Because that is the case, you may feel helpless in your desire to see your child get the best education possible. *After all,* you think, *it's out of my hands.* But ask yourself this simple question: Could a Congress, state legislature, or school board dictate that my children will be internally disciplined, respect their elders, go to bed early, and finish their homework? Who can teach those things to your children? No state body can legislate that you will spend time with your children, nurture their budding abilities, restrict their television viewing, and teach them what is truly valuable in life. You are the most important component in their education. Each teacher comes into their lives for a quarter, semester, or year, and then is gone. You, however, are with them throughout their lives. Even when faced with the challenge of a difficult or inferior teacher, you can create a positive public school experience.

What's Ahead for You

Let me outline what each chapter will cover for you. The following list is arranged by chapter and includes the questions or concerns that each chapter deals with.

Knowing Yourself

Chapter 2 will introduce you to ten major areas for helping your child develop, which I call Parent Power Tools. It is important that you spend some time assessing how well you currently use these tools. Chapter 2 gives you a test to help you do that.

Relating to Your Child's Teacher

It is, of course, natural to be concerned about the teacher or teachers your child will have in school. Since teachers are only human, they are subject to all the foibles and follies inherent in all of us. Public schools are also full of highly dedicated and gifted teachers who can help your child tremendously. Chapter 3 will help you work with the teacher in positive partnership. If you are worried about your relationship with the teacher, this chapter addresses the following concerns:

- How do I start off on the right foot with the teacher?
- What do I do if I don't approve of what the teacher is doing?
- What if I'm intimidated during parent-teacher conferences?
- How can I find time for parent-teacher conferences?

- What if the teacher's attitude or actions cause real problems?
- Will the teacher give my child the attention he needs?

Understanding the "Culture" of Your Child's School

School culture involves the overall environment within the school, its jargon, values, leadership, and customs. When your child attends a public school, he encounters people who have different—even opposing—values from your family's. For example, Lisa is the mother of a second-grader. She worries that the teacher will not enforce the standards she has set for her child. "I've met with the teacher and explained the expectations I have for Ashley. But I worry that if she steps outside my limits, the teacher—who might not fully agree with my values—will not correct her. Whereas chapter 3 shows you how to work with the teacher, chapter 4 helps you understand the culture of your school and how to guide your child through the differences between the values in your home and the values at school. The chapter will specifically help you with the following:

- What does the school consider a good value?
- Will someone pressure my child to conform to the school's values?
- Is my child's teacher going to push a political agenda?
- How do I teach my child discernment about what he hears at school?
- How do I talk to teachers and administrators if I have a serious objection to a value they are teaching?

Helping Your Child Develop Character and Withstand Peer Pressure

The influence of your child's peers on his or her attitudes and behavior could cause you to lose sleep. Will he develop good character qualities and stand up for what is right? Chapter 5 shows how to boost your child's character and deal with issues such as:

- Will my child be irresponsible?
- Will he get pressured into drinking, smoking, or using drugs?
- Will he think it is not "cool" to do well academically?
- How do I keep my child from being negatively influenced by peer pressure?
- Will he grow up to be a good person who makes wise decisions?
- Will he have healthy self-esteem?

Dealing with Concerns About Academic Success

All kinds of worries could flood over you with regard to how well your child will do academically. In any profession, some people are more gifted at what they do than others, and the teaching profession is no different. Your child may have a wonderful teacher, or he may have one that is not so good. The good news is that *you* can make a big difference in your child's academic success. Chapters 6, 7, 8, 9, and 12 will show you how to address the following challenges:

- What do I do if my child isn't motivated to learn?
- How can I best help my child do homework?
- How can I help if I don't know very much about certain academic subjects?
- How do I know if my child is reading at the appropriate grade level?
- What can I do if my child is a poor reader?
- How do I get my child away from the television set?
- Will my child be a bright and clear thinker in class, or will she be slow and sloppy?
- Will he speak up in class or be too shy to participate?
- How can I help my child become a better listener?
- How can I help my child stay focused on important goals?

Assisting Your Child's Spiritual Growth

Progressing academically without growing spiritually will leave your child unprepared to deal with many of life's problems. A healthy spiritual life can temper the flames of raw ambition and stem the pursuit of unworthy goals. But your child's spiritual growth can stall or be stunted during his education. Chapter 10 shows you how to create a spiritual curriculum at home and how to deal with the following worries:

- Will he have a strong faith at school?
- Will he be influenced by another set of beliefs in teachers or peers?
- How can I help him grow spiritually?

Having Adequate Family Time

At first you may be relieved that your first-grader's departure for school gives you a little personal space at home. Many parents, after playing recreational director all summer, are anxious for school to start and for their kids to get out of the house and back into the classroom. But even then there are things that require attention. Chapter 11 will help you overcome worries such as:

- Will our family time be crowded out by school activities?
- What can we do to counteract today's pop culture influence?
- How can I have significant conversations with my teenager?
- What activities can we do as a family?

Summary

These days there are a lot of things to worry about when you put your children in public schools. That's the bad news. The good news is that there are many things you can do to have greater assurance that your children will develop academically, morally, and spiritually.

It doesn't matter whether you have young children or teenagers. There are things you can do right now to maximize their education.

Imagine years from now hearing your son telling a friend: "My dad was never really into anything I did in school until junior high school. Something clicked into gear then, and I remember that year as the starting point for the best father-son relationship I could have wanted."

Or imagine your daughter years from now telling her friend: "My mother was really involved in my education. We had the best time together. Our relationship was always really strong. She made sure I used every ounce of my ability. Everything I am today is a tribute to her guidance."

This can happen for you. The appendix contains an implementation program. In thirty days you can put ten basic tools for successfully enhancing your children's education into use. Once you read this book, you are only thirty days away from turning your apprehension about public schools into excitement. You will be creating a positive public school experience.

Let's begin by looking at ten essential "power tools" for maximizing your children's education.

2
Know Yourself

Evaluate Yourself in Ten Key Areas That Affect Your Child.

The first step in getting where you want to go is knowing where to start. A little self-evaluation is good for determining how well you are currently using ten essential keys to help your child. When you finish this chapter, you will have a good idea where you need to focus your attention. These power tools are actions you can take to get the most for your child in his or her school—and there's plenty of good you can find there! The tools empower you to take greater charge of your child's academic, moral, and spiritual development. After considering how completely (or incompletely) you have developed these ten areas in the past, you will have a better idea of where to focus your attention in the future.

This chapter is divided into ten sections covering the ten Parent Power Tools. Each section has four categories that describe different levels of proficiency in using that power tool. Read each section, and decide which description fits you best *right now*. It is important that you be honest in your self-evaluation and think about what you are actually doing in relation to each power tool rather than what you would like to be doing. The answers will reveal strengths and weaknesses in your present ways of helping your child succeed. Don't be afraid of a low grade. The fact that you are reading this book is a big step toward improving your influence on your child's public education.

As you read the following descriptions, you may find that you don't fit neatly into one category; you may fall between two. That's fine. At the end of the section, when you are asked to give the number of the description that best fits you, simply indicate that you fall between two by adding a .5 to the lower number. For instance, you may feel that you are between description 2 and description 3. In that case, write 2.5 for your answer.

The Ten Parent Power Tools	
1.	Know the teacher.
2.	Understand the culture of your child's school.
3.	Encourage your child at home.
4.	Display interest in your child's subject.
5.	Maximize reading at home.
6.	Monitor the amount of television you watch.
7.	Promote thinking skills through conversation.
8.	Emphasize spiritual growth.
9.	Promote family togetherness.
10.	Establish goals as a family.

Parent Power Tool #1:
Know the Teacher.

A vital first step toward helping your child is communicating with his teacher. You and the teacher are a team. You must work together. In my years of working with parents, I have seen a wide range of attitudes toward teachers. On one extreme are parents who are completely ignorant of what happens at school. They are too busy with other pursuits to follow what is happening in class. On the other end of the spectrum are those parents who are constantly suspicious of the teacher. They look at everything the teacher does with a wary eye. When they hear about a new activity the teacher is beginning, they wonder, *What's her real agenda?* The common factor between the parents on both extremes is their lack of engagement with the teacher. One is disengaged because of apathy, the other because of fear.

The most effective parent is the one who makes a special effort at building a solid relationship with the teacher. This parent understands and promotes the team concept. The key distinction between this parent and the others described above is that this parent takes initiative. To fit into this category, you need to initiate parent-teacher communication. It may take the form of notes, letters, conferences, in-class volunteering, or a telephone call to the teacher. Frequent communication is es-sential.

Not only is the *quantity* of your communication important, but the *quality* is as well. When you communicate with the teacher you need to develop a keen sense of her values and methods as well as an understanding of the content of her lessons. Building a relationship with the teacher means you have a greater grasp of what she is doing and why. Choose the description below that describes your present teamwork with your child's teacher.

Description 1

I have never met with my child's teacher. I never communicate with the teacher regarding my child's progress.

(If your child is in junior or senior high school, this applies to all of his or her teachers. The teacher may communicate with you, but the issue is whether you communicate with the teacher.)

Description 2

I attend school open house and attend parent-teacher conferences when asked. I do meet with the teacher, but I do not initiate those meetings.

Description 3

I have some idea of what the teacher's values and methods are. I communicate occasionally with the teacher to find out how my child is doing.

Description 4

I initiate regular meetings with all adults involved in my child's education. We discuss specific and positive ways to enhance my child's progress. I know the values of the teacher. We are a team allied against problems.

· The description that fits me best for Parent Power Tool #1 is _____. (Remember, you may fall between two descriptions.)

Parent Power Tool #2: Understand the Culture of Your Child's School.

Your child's school's culture is made up of many things that give the school a unique flavor. Understanding the various ingredients that create that flavor is important for comprehending the kind of environment your child lives in during the day. This involves knowing the right person to go to when you have a problem, being sensitive to factors within the district that may affect the way teachers and administrators in the school respond to you, and knowing the school's beliefs, jargon, and methods well enough to translate them for your child's understanding. (By "jargon" I mean the terms that instructors and administrators use when talking about educational techniques and policies.) Picture yourself as a tour director for your child in the school culture. How well can you guide her through the maze of new experiences she will encounter?

Description 1

I don't know how things get done in the school system. I believe, for the most part, that my responsibility for my child is in the home and the school is responsible for his education.

Description 2

I would like to know how to get what I want from the school, but I have never initiated any action for learning how to do that.

Description 3

I understand the roles of school personnel and have, on occasion, used that knowledge to intercede for my child. I don't make it a habit to keep up on the methods of instruction or the content of my child's classes.

Description 4

I know who to talk to about a particular issue. I am sensitive to the personalities and politics in the system. I know how to present myself. I understand the beliefs, values, methods, content, and jargon that school personnel use in conjunction with my child's education and regularly discuss those with my child.

The description that best fits me for Parent Power Tool #2 is ____.

Parent Power Tool #3: Encourage Your Child at Home.

Encouragement at home is an important success-builder for your child. Unfortunately, many parents do not encourage their children enough. It may be that they believe that too much encouragement will spoil a child. It could be that they feel awkward about encouraging their children. Though they want to encourage them, they find that they do not. When evaluating yourself, be honest in assessing how much you actually say words of encouragement to your child. Do not count your intent or the pride you feel about your child but don't express.

The parent who encourages a child is one who looks for opportunities to make affirming statements about the child's abilities, attitudes, or character and then does it.

Description 1

I rarely say anything positive about my child's abilities, attitudes, or character.

Description 2

I want to affirm my child more but find it difficult to say a lot of positive things about my child's abilities, attitudes, or character because there seem to be so few opportunities.

Description 3

I really praise my child when he does a good job. If he fails at something, I usually don't say anything one way or the other.

Description 4

I look for opportunities to make affirming statements about my child's abilities, attitudes, or character. I give my child lots of encouragement throughout each week.

The description that best fits me for Parent Power Tool #3 is ____.

Parent Power Tool #4: Display Interest in Your Child's Subject.

Learning the subject their children are studying is often overlooked by parents as they get involved in their children's education. If you really want to help your child learn more effectively, this is an important ingredient. It means going beyond merely getting after your child to do his homework. It even goes beyond helping your child do his homework. It requires that you read up on the subject, that you look for opportunities to talk about the subject, and that you show enthusiasm for the subject yourself.

This is so uncommon for parents to do that I will not be surprised if you choose description 1 or 2 below. If this is true for you, don't feel bad. The road to improvement starts with a realistic assessment of where you are right now.

Description 1

I don't really know what my child learns at school except in general categories (history, English, math, etc.).

Description 2

I ask my child what she is learning in school, and we occasionally discuss it. I see my role as making sure she gets her homework done.

Description 3

I show enthusiasm for each subject my child is studying. I ask him what he is learning, and we discuss it. I point out to him practical applications for the learning.

Description 4

I read up on the subjects my child is studying. I look for real-world applications of his studies. I read his textbooks or get extra copies for myself. I am genuinely enthusiastic about each subject.

The description that best fits me for Parent Power Tool #4 is _____.

Parent Power Tool #5: Maximize Reading at Home.

We all recognize the importance of reading for academic success. However, too often reading is not a priority in families. Reading aloud doesn't have to be just for children. You might be surprised to find that there are ways you can read to teenagers and your spouse as well. Have you ever sipped coffee on a Saturday morning with your spouse while you both read the newspaper? Occasionally you might run across an interesting article and read it out loud for your spouse's benefit. That is similar to how you can read to an older child or young person. At dinner you can read a short magazine article, a passage of Scripture, or a thought for the day from an interesting book. Do you do this?

Reading doesn't just involve books. You can read magazines, newspapers, even comic books. Of course, there should be a good mixture of types and levels of reading. Take a realistic assessment of how much time you spend reading in your family.

Description 1

Reading isn't a real priority in our home. I seldom read to my child.

Description 2

I read to my child about once each week. I don't see my child reading much at home.

Description 3

I read to my child frequently, and I encourage him to read for pleasure.

Description 4

Everyone in the family is reading something nearly every day. We talk about what we are reading, and I read to my child regularly and frequently. We demonstrate that reading is valuable.

The description that best fits me for Parent Power Tool #5 is ____.

Parent Power Tool #6: Monitor the Amount of Television You Watch.

Television is not only a powerful distraction from more important things, but it also conditions children's thinking skills in ways that can hinder good learning. It is not uncommon to underestimate the amount of television we watch. It may be that we feel a slight bit of guilt over sitting in front of the electronic box for so long each night. Because of that, it is easy to brush off your television viewing as insignificant.

After all, we think, *I don't watch as much as So-and-so does.*

To help you be objective on this, use your weekly television listings. Read the listing of television programs for the last few days and circle the programs you watched. It should take less than ten minutes to do. Add up the hours you watched. You may be surprised. You may watch a longer program or sports event one afternoon yet not watch any television the next day. I've listed both daily and weekly viewing amounts to accommodate this.

Description 1

The TV is on for more than four hours each day or more than twenty-eight hours each week.

Description 2

The TV is on between two and four hours each day or fourteen to twenty-eight hours each week.

Description 3

The TV is on for about one hour each day or seven hours each week.

Description 4

The TV is on for only thirty minutes each day or three and one-half hours each week.

(Give yourself a bonus point if you got rid of the TV.)

The description that best fits me for Parent Power Tool #6 is ____.

Parent Power Tool #7: Promote Thinking Skills Through Conversation.

Conversations with your child are important for three reasons: they create emotional well-being, teach the child how to interact socially, and develop academic thinking skills. As you evaluate the quality of your conversations with your child, you need to distinguish between conversation and directives. In short, that is the difference between talking *with* someone and talking *to* him. Directives or instructions often have to do with maintaining household things ("Don't leave your bike in the driveway," or, "Please go with your sister to the store"). Conversations involve things about which there can be a dialogue. They are like a tennis game. Each side has to return the ball in order for the game to be any fun. In evaluating the quality of your conversations, you can look at how much back-and-forth communication occurs. A conversation doesn't have to be an intense talk about intimate things. It can be light, short, and fun. But each person needs to share the responsibility of creating the dialogue.

Description 1

We seldom have prolonged conversations about what is happening in each others lives. Mostly, I give my child instructions or directives.

Description 2

I generally have a prolonged conversation with my child only when he is going through a problem in his life.

Description 3

I make it a point to have conversational time together with my child. We do talk a lot, but the conversations seem to be just surface topics. I wish we could have more significant talks.

Description 4

We have great conversations about what is happening each day in our lives. We talk about problems and successes. We even discuss news events. We share equally in carrying the conversation.

The description that best fits me for Parent Power Tool #7 is _____.

Parent Power Tool #8: Emphasize Spiritual Growth.

Education is about more than learning facts, figures, and skills. It is about refining your values and answering the bigger questions of life. This requires living what some have called the examined life—the life that reflects on deeper issues. I often wonder where a student whose family does not attend religious services receives spiritual input. When does she examine her life? She sleeps in on the weekends while others are going to their places of worship and are being challenged to think about the deeper issues of life. When is she ever challenged to think, in any intelligent way, about God, eternity, prayer, or the higher callings of man? It is quite possible for children in spiritually deprived homes to grow up without ever seriously examining their lives.

Think for a moment on the amount and quality of spiritual reflection in your home. Is this an important area of your life? Have you ever talked about your beliefs with your child? Have you made an effort to help her grow in spiritual depth? Think about those questions as you find the description below that best fits you.

Description 1

We really don't talk about spiritual things.

Description 2

I make sure my child attends religious services, but I don't regularly attend.

Description 3

We regularly attend religious services as a family and pretty much let our place of worship guide our family's spiritual development.

Description 4

We not only attend services together, but we actively set spiritual growth goals and seek ways to accomplish those spiritual milestones.

The description that best fits me for Parent Power Tool #8 is ____.

Parent Power Tool #9: Promote Family Togetherness.

Strong family bonds can give solid foundations for a child's academic and social success. These bonds are built through spending quality time together. The quantity of time you spend together as a family has much to do with the quality of the time vou spend. Certainly you can spend lots of time together in the same room without it being quality time. Watching television together all evening is an example of how that can happen. However, quantity affords greater opportunities for quality. The more time you spend together, the more opportunities you have to create intimacy, to capitalize on the teachable moment, and to act as a good role model for your child.

Reflect on the amount of time you spend together in relationship-enriching activities. The activities could be almost anything, such as shopping, recreation, hobbies, or playing games. They could even include chores done together, such as gardening, painting, or repairing the car.

Description 1

We spend less than one hour each week in a family activity such as a game, hobby, or outing.

Description 2

We spend between one and two hours each week in a family activity.

Description 3

We spend between two and three hours each week in a family activity.

Description 4

We spend more than three hours each week in a family activity.

The description that best fits me for Parent Power Tool #9 is ____.

Parent Power Tool #10: Establish Goals as a Family.

Goals are important for creating a sense of purpose, direction, and accomplishment in life. When you ponder exactly what your goals should be, you must take a look at the big picture. The very act of prioritizing long-range goals helps you create a sense of purpose. To a lesser degree, this also happens when your child prioritizes his goals. Planning his goals requires him to reflect on the many roles he plays (as English student, history student, math student, Boy Scout, son, brother, etc.). The goals within roles create a greater sense of purpose.

Goals give you direction. When you establish a specific goal, you are, by definition, excluding an infinite number of other options. You are creating focus in your life. As your child does this, he too will experience the calming effect of having a clearly definable direction.

It is important that your child have many successes throughout the week. When he sets and strives toward a goal, he has created a success for himself. For your developing child, this may be the most important product of goal setting.

Take an honest look at the role of goals in your family as you find the description that best fits you.

Description 1

I don't emphasize established goals with my child.

Description 2

My child has a general idea of what he wants to accomplish, but we have not written them down. My child is not making a focused effort toward reaching his general ideas.

Description 3

We have discussed several goals but have not written them down. However, my child generally moves toward accomplishing those mental goals.

Description 4

My child has several clearly defined and written goals and is actively progressing toward their accomplishment. We encourage goal setting with our child.

The description that best fits me for Parent Power Tool #10 is _____.

That was a lot of work! You now have the information about your strengths and weaknesses you need to help your child have a positive public school experience. Now, let's make some use of your effort.

REPORT CARD	**Parent Power Tool Scoring**	
	Transfer your scores to the ten blanks below:	
	1.	Know the teacher.
	2.	Understand the culture of your child's school.
	3.	Encourage your child at home.
	4.	Display interest in your child's subject.
	5.	Maximize reading at home.
	6.	Monitor the amount of television you watch.
	7.	Promote thinking skills through conversation.
	8.	Emphasize spiritual growth.
	9.	Promote family togetherness.
	10.	Establish goals as a family.

Interpreting Your Score

Power Tool #1: Know the Teacher.

If you fit description 1, chapter 3 will help you tremendously. Give special attention to how to communicate with the teacher. This is an important area and you need to give it a higher priority.

If you fit description 2, you are too passive in managing your child's classroom progress. You are not taking charge of your child's education. Chapter 3 will show you how to have more effective parent-teacher meetings.

If you fit description 3, you are not yet a full partner with your child's teacher. Increase the frequency of your communication. Chapter 3 gives suggestions on how to write notes to the teacher that will help your child.

If you fit description 4, you are on top of your child's school experience. You may need to simply record your parent-teacher interaction so you can track your child's progress better. Chapter 3 can help you deal with a problem teacher.

Power Tool #2: Understand the Culture of Your Child's School.

If you fit description 1, you may feel schools can be intimidating or mystifying, but you need to understand them better. Your child's success depends on it. Chapter 4 has several suggestions for helping you start right away.

If you fit description 2, it is good that you desire to learn more about the school. Now, get going! Intentions without actions are useless. You are still "out of the loop". Chapter 4 can help you get inside it.

If you fit description 3, you are doing a good job. However, new methods of instruction are flooding the classroom, so you must work to stay current in understanding them. Chapter 4 will explain some of those new trends and give you direction in understanding your own school.

If you fit description 4, outstanding! You are truly in a position to guide your child through the maze of school. But instruction methods, jargon, and content can change rapidly, so remember to stay current. Chapter 4 gives you three techniques for using your knowledge to intercede for your child.

Power Tool #3: Encourage Your Child at Home.

If you fit description 1, you are at risk of hindering your child's development if you do not encourage him more. Read chapter 5 carefully, and start using the encouragement techniques explained there.

If you fit description 2, you are not looking very hard if you think there aren't enough positive things to encourage in your child. Chapter 5 offers a specific way for you to uncover all kinds of positive things about your child.

If you fit description 3, remember, praise is different from encouragement. You obviously have a good attitude about your child's behavior, but you need to learn to be an encourager. Chapter 5 will help you with this. It will also help you know how to correct your child's mistakes in a positive way.

If you fit description 4, outstanding! You are actively shaping your child's self-confidence and healthy self-image. You may need to simply expand the number of qualities you encourage in your child. Chapter 5 lists many qualities that you may not normally attach to your child. It can open up entirely new avenues for building up your child.

Power Tool #4: Display Interest in Your Child's Subject

If you fit description 1, you are missing an important opportunity for shaping your child's attitudes toward learning. Your lack of interest may have a negative influence on your child. Chapter 6 will show you easy ways to demonstrate an interest in what your child learns.

If you fit description 2, your child may do her homework more enthusiastically if you show a greater interest in her learning. You are too passive. You could do much more to help your child develop enthusiasm and curiosity for a subject. Chapter 6 will give you many good ideas for enhancing your school-related conversation with your child.

If you fit description 3, your enthusiasm will enhance your child's learning attitude, and the real-world application you point out to him will bring meaning to each subject. You need only work on being a role model for active learning in your own life. Chapter 6 will show you how to do that.

If you fit description 4, wonderful! You are modeling for your child that learning is important. You can get some new ideas from chapter 6.

Power Tool #5: Maximize Reading at Home

If you fit description 1, uh-oh! Turn off the TV, and go buy two magazines and a newspaper right now! At least you are reading this book. Chapter 7 gives you many ideas on how to make reading a bigger part of your home.

If you fit description 2, increase the frequency of your reading to your child. Consider reading a short poem, article, or Scripture during dinner that will prompt discussion. Chapter 7 will show you how to use the library more.

If you fit description 3, good job. However, you can model the importance and pleasure of reading by letting your child see you reading on a regular basis. Chapter 7 can help you encourage greater reading comprehension in your child.

If you fit description 4, great job! Reading is obviously a high priority in your home, and you are modeling it to your child. Chapter 7 gives you a way to measure your child's reading level and exercises that will increase his skills.

Power Tool #6: Monitor the Amount of Television You Watch

If you fit description 1, you are a couch potato and are raising little french fries! Chapter 8 will show you why excessive TV viewing can be detrimental to your child's development.

If you fit description 2, you are missing out on a lot of real things you could be doing at home and as a family. Chapter 8 will help you think of activities that can help replace the TV.

If you fit description 3, good. You are demonstrating that TV is not a priority. Chapter 8 will help you watch TV with a discerning eye.

If you fit description 4, great! You are firmly in control of the media culture's invasion of your home. Chapter 8 will give you new insight as to the importance of your decision to limit TV viewing.

Power Tool #7: Promote Thinking Skills Through Conversation

If you fit description 1, you are missing opportunities to shape your child's values and attitudes, as well as to bond with her. Chapter 9 will give you specific questions to ask your child that promote conversations.

If you fit description 2, it is good that you are able to talk with your child about problems, but you need to make conversation with your child a greater part of your daily interaction. You may need to write conversation time on your daily to-do list. Chapter 9 will show you the four keys to having wonderful conversations.

If you fit description 3, you have obviously made communication a priority but now need to do some thinking in advance on what to talk about. With a little more effort in your conversations, you can make a world of difference for your child socially, emotionally, and academically. Chapter 9 will show you how to use conversation to promote thinking skills.

If you fit description 4, outstanding! You are helping your child develop into a real thinker! Chapter 9 will give you specific thinking skill-building conversations.

Power Tool #8: Emphasize Spiritual Growth

If you fit description 1, you are neglecting a major area of your child's life. Chapter 10 explains why the spiritual side of your child's development is important.

If you fit description 2, your child is probably assuming that spiritual growth is not important based on your example. Chapter 10 explains why your spiritual views are so vital to your child's.

If you fit description 3, you are doing a good job of helping your child develop spiritually on a once-per-week basis, but what do you do during the week at home? Expand the time you spend on spiritual growth and incorporate it in your week. Chapter 10 offers specific subjects you can think about and talk about throughout the week.

If you fit description 4, outstanding! You are actively engaged in coaching your child to grow spiritually. Chapter 10 offers you a new way of describing to your child what it means to be a child of the King.

Power Tool #9: Promote Family Togetherness.

If you fit description 1, you are missing opportunities with your child. Consider taking a hard look at your schedule and trying to find something to drop from your calendar. Chapter 11 explains why time with your family is so important to your child's development.

If you fit description 2, rearrange your schedule, and make a few cuts where necessary. Chapter 11 offers many ideas for family activities.

If you fit description 3, good. You are making family time a priority. Now begin spending more time with your child one-on-one. Chapter 11 explains ways to create family traditions and unique stories.

If you fit description 4, tremendous! You are not only setting aside time for your family, you are investing in personal development with your child. Chapter 11 suggests creative additions to your family activities.

Power Tool #10: Establish Goals as a Family.

If you fit description 1, you are letting circumstances dictate your child's life too much. Chapter 12 explains why goal setting is important to your child's school success.

If you fit description 2, plans without actions are not goals—they are dreams. Help your child be more specific with his ideas and attach action steps to them. Chapter 12 will help him learn the skill of goal setting.

If you fit description 3, have your child write down her goals, and post them in a prominent place. Chapter 12 shows you the three ingredients for successful goal accomplishment.

If you fit description 4, wonderful! Your child is living life with purpose rather than by accident. Chapter 12 suggests a variety of new areas you might consider setting goals for.

Summary

The inventory you have just completed is, of course, not scientific. It does, however, serve as a starting point as you reflect on ten essential areas that affect your child's education and development. You have taken an important step in creating a positive public school experience for your child—in the process of completing this evaluation, you have begun thinking about your involvement in your child's education in an entirely new light. You should now have a greater sense of focus and direction in what you need to do.

The first step in maximizing your child's education is to build a good relationship with your educational partner—the teacher. And that is where we will start in the next chapter.

3

Get Acquainted

Parent Power Tool #1: Know the Teacher

Your Goal
I initiate regular meetings with all adults involved in my child's education. We discuss positive and specific ways to enhance my child's progress. I know the values of the teacher. We are a team allied against problems.

Your child's education is like a jump rope—it takes two people working in unison to keep him hopping. You and your child's teacher must work in unison to maximize his education. This chapter is designed to give you one thing: a relationship with the teacher that is best for your child. You want to know how to maximize parent-teacher relations to get an outstanding education for your child right now. Relating to your child's teacher doesn't have to be a burden. It can be fun. And your child will be the real winner when you and the teacher get together.

Perhaps you have not set foot inside a school since your graduation. Presently, you may not communicate with your child's teacher at all. But after reading this chapter and implementing it, you could receive an award for outstanding parent of the year from that educator. And you will be able to do it while investing less time than you might imagine.

Envision a Team

Let's start with the problem. If you have no relationship with the teacher, you have no partnership either. No partnership means your child loses, because there is no coordinated educational experience for him. Begin right now to see yourself as a team member with the teacher. In fact, you are the most important member of the team! Your child spends only about a third of the day with school personnel and the other sixteen hours under your influence. You are the only person in your child's life who is a constant presence. The teacher is there for only nine months or one semester. When you are not actively participating as a team member with the teacher, you are severely handicapping the teacher and limiting the opportunities for your child.

You know better than anyone what makes your child happy, sad, excited, or afraid. You know what she is interested in and what she finds boring. You know what is going on in the family and among her friends that affects her emotions and her learning. But most of all, she looks to you more than anyone else for significance, approval, and encouragement. Walking away from your role as team member is like leaving the teacher holding one end of a jump rope with your child standing in the middle. To be a team player you need to take the initiative in building a positive relationship.

Establish a Relationship

Step 1: Getting Started

To paraphrase Dale Carnegie, you will find it easy to make friends when you are sincerely interested in other people. It is difficult to make friends by trying to get people interested in you. People are always more attracted to others who are interested in them, and teachers are no different than anyone else.

Some parents approach teachers like the egocentric socialite who, after going on and on about himself, stated, "Well, enough of me talking about myself. What do you think of me?" The teacher spends all day, every day, thinking about your child. When you begin communicating with the teacher, you need to show interest in the teacher. Start by sending a note to the teacher this week. The note should be affirming and focused on the teacher. Comment on something he or she did that you like; for example, "Your lesson on the ocean was great. Johnny talked about it for days! Keep up the good work." Don't give false praise. Find something the teacher has done on which you can genuinely compliment him or her.

Did the teacher foster a new enthusiasm for learning in your child?

Did the teacher help your child overcome a learning difficulty?

Did the teacher give a lesson your child particularly enjoyed?

Did the teacher show extra care in helping your child?

Did the teacher give detailed feedback on her homework?

Sending an affirming note to the teacher costs you pennies and it takes less than one minute to write. Yet the effect is monumental. Think about when you last received a note from someone expressing appreciation for something you did. Didn't it make you feel great?

People become teachers because they want to make a difference in kids' lives. They certainly are not teaching because of the money or because they enjoy the stress. So when you let your son's teacher know she did something that made a difference, she is uplifted. When she is uplifted, she teaches with more enthusiasm. And she will appreciate you because you helped her to remember why she got into teaching in the first place. She may even give just a little more attention to your child's needs because she knows the effort she invests will be supported and appreciated by you.

A personal contact to express your appreciation for the teacher will make a dramatic impact. Bob and Nancy of Riverside, California, are examples of parents who go out of their way to build a good relationship with the teacher. They invite each of their children's teachers home for dinner. They commented that the teachers appreciate the invitation, and it helps the children learn to respect their teachers and show appreciation for them.

Step 2: Lend a Hand

After you have written a note or two demonstrating that you are a team member with the teacher, write another type of note. This note is an offer to help with something. Be specific:

"I understand that _____ is coming up. Please call me if I can help."

It is less likely that the teacher will call you if you simply offer your help without attaching it to a specific event or project. The teacher may be reluctant to ask for help or impose on someone, but if you offer to help on a specific project, you allow the teacher a graceful way to accept your help without feeling like she is forcing you to do something you don't want to do.

There are many ways you can lend a helping hand to a teacher:

- Volunteer to be a field trip chaperone or help with the logistics.
- Read with a student.
- Call parents to set up a special event or remind them of a field trip.
- Demonstrate a hobby to the class.
- Be a guest lecturer on a topic the class is learning about and in which you have experience.
- Videotape an educational program for classroom use when the teacher isn't able to.
- Help set up lab materials for a science lesson.
- Help make things at home that the teacher can use in class, such as cutout letters for bulletin boards.

Remember, the key is to be more interested in what the teacher is doing than in what you get out of the relationship right now. In any relationship you must earn the right to be heard. You may protest, "My taxes pay that teacher's salary, and she is hired to teach my son. I have the right to be heard. I don't need to earn it!" Technically, you may be right. But in the real world of egos and emotions, people open up to you when you have demonstrated that being open is important and valuable.

Most elementary school teachers will gladly welcome your involvement. Be aware that some teachers may not be used to an actively involved parent with a team-player mentality. Some teachers are so used to apathetic parents that they don't know what to do with an enthusiastic one. If you find yourself in that situation, give the relationship time and win the teacher's heart.

Teachers at the high school level are not used to much parent involvement. Secondary schools have a different atmosphere largely due to a combination of the students being older and the fact that they spend only one hour a day with each teacher. Still, you can build a constructive relationship with each of your child's teachers. Here are five things you can do in your child's middle school or high school:

- Be sure to attend every open house to meet the teachers. It may be that so few parents attend these at your school that you will stand out in each teacher's mind.
- Occasionally send an encouraging and appreciative note to the teacher.
- Offer to be a guest speaker to the class if you have a relevant expertise. For instance, if you work with computers, your teenager's math teacher might like you to tell the class about your experience. Brian, a high school economics teacher in southern California, told me about a mother who worked at a bank and visited his class to explain how a bank functioned. "It really added an interesting perspective to the subject," he said.
- If you don't have expertise in the subject, offer to contact a friend or relative who does. "Sometimes I want to find someone who is an expert in a certain aspect of business," said Brian, "and a parent will have a friend who is willing to address the class."
- Get involved with the school's PTA. This will give you school-wide visibility, and teachers will appreciate you. They will get to know you and respect you for your involvement.

Step 3: Address Your Child's Specific Needs

When I list these three steps, I do not mean that you cannot talk about your child's needs without first sending three complimentary notes and volunteering in the classroom. Obviously, if your child has a need in the classroom that must be addressed right away, do it. However, you can still use a condensed version of steps one and two. If you must meet with the teacher to discuss a concern with your child early in the school year, start the meeting with an affirmation of the teacher, mention that you want to help on a specific project or event, and *then* talk about your child's need. Though you haven't had time to build a relationship of trust and mutual respect with the teacher, she will sense that you are a team member and probably will be more open to your concern.

When writing a note of concern to the teacher, try the sandwich approach. Sandwich your concern between a positive opening and closing. For instance, if you are concerned that your child is not getting enough feedback on homework assignments, you might write the following:

Dear Mrs. Smith,

Jim has been enjoying your lessons on weather patterns. We make a point of watching the weatherman every night now, and Jim is more motivated to do his homework. It would help us both a great deal if you could write more detailed feedback on his assignments about where he needs to improve. Thanks in advance for doing this, and keep up the excellent work.

When you address your child's specific need, avoid sounding like you are accusing the teacher. No one likes to be dumped on. Try to use "I" statements such as, "I feel uncomfortable with . . . " or "I don't understand why . . ." or "My experience has been that Johnny doesn't respond well to . . ." Following these three steps will go a long way toward developing a partnership with your teacher. Sometimes, though, you will have concerns that are too complicated to be conveyed in a note, and you will need to have a conference with the teacher.

Having Terrific
Parent-Teacher Conferences

Conferences with the teacher can cause anxiety. It is easy to be intimidated when you feel that your skills as a parent are being judged. In my experience, however, the teacher often feels the same way—that her skills as a teacher are being evaluated. Many teachers dread parent-teacher conferences more than the parents do. For some it's like having their work reviewed by all the parents in the classroom. Other teachers dread having to talk to parents about their child's poor progress or behavior. Here are six simple guidelines to help you have terrific meetings.

Lay the Right Groundwork. As outlined above, build a friendly, teammate relationship with the teacher early in the school year. If you have laid the right groundwork, both you and the teacher will feel more at ease in the meeting.

It is important to know what the meeting is about. What will be discussed? Is this a routine meeting or a special meeting to address a particular problem? Who will be there—just the teacher, or the school psychologist or an administrator as well? It is a good idea to develop a list of questions before you come to the meeting. List those questions you need to ask to help your child's educational progress.

Have the Right Attitude. Come to the meeting as a team member, not as a parent competing with the teacher for the future of your child. View the teacher as someone with children of her own—a parent just like you. Don't be intimidated. You are the team leader regarding your child's overall development. Of course, you don't need to convey that to the teacher. That would only cause the teacher to feel as if you are competing for power. Instead, rest in the confidence that you remain your child's educational coach for many years, spanning many different teachers. You are the one who must coordinate his learning experiences throughout his schooling. You can see things in your child that the teacher cannot. She depends on you to provide that kind of leadership in your relationship.

Also, do not feel unwelcome if your child has a discipline problem at school. Make your child's discipline a team effort. One teacher told me, "Some of the parents I am closest with are those who have problem kids. Sometimes we both just chuckle and say, 'There he goes again.' But it has drawn us closer."

Wear the Right Attire. Come to the meeting dressed as if you are going to work at the office. Look professional. That will have a positive effect on the teacher's attitude toward you. A friendship is forged through mutual respect. If the teacher sees you dressed sloppily, she may perceive you as a sloppy parent. Her respect for you may decrease, and you'll have a lopsided relationship.

Have the Right Focus: Accentuate the Positive. One elementary school teacher told me, "I love it when parents tell me positive things about their kids. It gives me an insight into the child that I might not have noticed." That is important. When you say positive things about your child, it will rub off on the teacher.

For instance, you might say, "Sally is so curious to discover new things at home." The next time Sally has a question in class, the teacher can't help viewing it as Sally's eagerness to learn. The teacher's body language, facial expressions, and verbal communication with Sally may change. Even if Sally's behavior does not always indicate an eagerness to learn, the teacher may think, *Underneath it all, she really enjoys learning. I know because her mom told me so.* Keep in mind, however, that your positive statements must be accurate. If you stretch the truth, the teacher will eventually assume that you are a poor judge of your own child and begin to disregard what you say.

It is also a good idea to ask the teacher to tell you something positive about your child. Simply say, "Tell me something Sally has done with which you are pleased." That will encourage the teacher to also focus on the positive in the meeting.

Have the Right Agenda. Your meeting should be about finding positive solutions to educational hurdles. You and the teacher are aligned together against problems. Try to spend only about 25 percent of the meeting talking about problems and 75 percent of the time outlining solutions. Solutions will involve discussing constructive action toward well-established learning goals, time management, monitoring progress, or adjusting some aspect of the school program to better meet your child's needs.[1]

Keep the meeting moving forward with a pleasant and relaxed let's-get-down-to-business approach. By planning ahead you will be able to set the pace for the meeting and convey that you are looking for constructive results, not casual conversation about your child. It will also establish your relationship with the teacher for future meetings. The teacher will realize that you take your role as an educational partner seriously.

Have the Right Conclusion. Conclude your meeting with clearly written goals for your child. Ask questions such as, "What are the current educational goals for my child? How can I monitor his progress? What can I do to help you achieve these goals?"[2] Also, end with a warm and affirming statement to the teacher. Express your appreciation for her work or tell her of a specific example of how she helped your child.

Finding the Time for Terrific Parent-Teacher Conferences

Finding the time for meeting with the teacher is always a challenge for parents who work outside the home. If it is a problem for you, don't let it deter you from having the meeting. Determine right now that you will have the meeting, then do whatever it takes to make it happen.

You make time for other things to interrupt your regular day. You make doctor and dentist appointments during the day. You take your car to the mechanic during the day. You take a break from work and go out to lunch. Your child's education is one of the most important things you can focus on. Be creative with your scheduling.

Meet during your lunch hour.
Meet before you go to work.

Meet after work.
Take half a day off of work.
Meet via the telephone.
Meet on a weekend.
Make up the hour you lost by working late one night.

Once you have a conference with the teacher and have determined what your child needs to do to succeed in the classroom, you can be more supportive of the teacher at home. You can actually become a co-teacher—monitoring your child's progress, helping him focus on his studies, and giving him opportunities to practice what he has learned.

Active Co-teaching

You are an educational partner with the teacher. *Together* you are teaching your child. To maximize your child's education you must see it as a team effort. Below are listed some ways you can actively co-teach your child: Work with your child at home, and organize your own field trip.

Work with Your Child at Home

Homework does two things for a student: It helps her learn, and it teaches responsibility. Here are five steps you can take at home to help your child learn better and faster and have greater retention. By using these techniques you are not only helping your child learn, but you are teaching her *how* to learn as well.

1. *Set Clear Learning Goals.* It is important that your child understand what he is supposed to get out of the lesson. Go beyond simple goals such as, "Read three pages." Instead, help him list things he will learn in those three pages using the chapter summaries, subheadings, and questions usually provided at the end of each section of the textbook. If the science topic is the cell, have him write down a few questions such as, "What is a cell? What is in a cell? What do

cells do?" That helps him read for meaning. He is searching for answers, not just covering pages. If the teacher assigned a worksheet of questions to be answered from the reading, he should read those questions before reading his textbook. Even then, it would be a good idea for him to write a summary statement clarifying what he will be learning from the worksheet; for example, "In this assignment I will learn about cells and what they do."

Strategy Tip: Have your child write or state a one-sentence summary to clarify why he is doing the lesson.

2. *Help Him Break the Homework into Logical Sequences of Learning.* What does he need to know first? What basic skill does he need to learn first to complete each task successfully? For instance, if he is learning about fractions, how are his division skills? Learning is progressive. One concept builds on another. One skill is learned after another. If there is a weak link in your child's learning, it can hinder his progress every time that weakness is needed. Mastery of each step is important for overall success.

For example, the assignment may be to write a two-page report on India. The child needs to know where to find appropriate source material on India (Step 1); this will vary with his grade level. Copying directly from an encyclopedia is a common, but poor, shortcut for many students. Instead, he needs to know how to use the library to check out one or two books on India. He can find facts on India's weather from an almanac. He can use bits of information on India's customs, government, and religion from an encyclopedia.

He will need to outline what he will write in his report (Step 2). As he finds information to fill each part of his outline, he should write that bit of information on a three-by-five card and make a notation at the top for where it fits into his outline (Step 3). Finally, he will need to write the report based on all the information on his note cards, but he must write the information in his own words unless he is making a direct quote (Step 4).

In this example, the student must have certain skills: using the library, outlining, categorizing research using three-by-five cards, and paraphrasing material in his own words. If he lacks any one of those skills, he may become frustrated and either compromise the quality of his report or quit altogether.

Strategy Tip: Ask your child to jot down or tell you the steps he will go through to complete this task.

3. *Give Her Concrete Examples That Illustrate the Lesson.* Most of us learn better when we have concrete examples to illustrate what we are studying. Students learn better when they can picture the point they are learning. With a little creativity you can help this happen. For example, when your child is learning about the executive branch of government, show her a picture of the White House. For a lesson on fractions, use slices of freshly baked pie. When studying about the atmosphere, watch the television weather report at night and point out various cloud formations during the day.

Strategy Tip: Help your child see how the lesson applies to the real world.

4. *Ask Questions That Force Him to Answer in His Own Words.* Instead of asking, "Do you understand?" to which he can simply answer yes or no, ask questions that require longer answers. When your child has to explain his answer, he processes what he has learned. If he cannot explain it in his own words, he

has not truly learned it. If, for example, your child is learning a new math procedure, ask him to teach you the procedure. Putting him in the role of the teacher requires that he understand the lesson in order to explain it.

Strategy Tip: Ask your child what he is learning and have him explain it to you.

5. *Give Him Frequent Opportunities to Practice What He Has Learned.* Your child may forget what he learns without frequent practice. You can use a variety of creative activities to help him practice his learning. For instance, use news events to help him review his geography lesson, or ask him to write a letter to a relative to practice his new vocabulary words.

Strategy Tip: Think about the topics your child is learning and try to find common applications so he can practice what he learns.

Organize Your Own Field Trip

You can organize your own field trip for your child as well as for the entire class. This is a great way to build a close relationship with the teacher. There is no rule that says parents cannot organize an extracurricular outing. Here's how to do it:

1. Come up with an idea for a Saturday activity that is related to something the students are learning.
2. Talk to the teacher about it, and see if it is something she would enjoy doing. Assure her that she will not have to do any work, nor will she have any liability, because each parent will be responsible for his or her own child. This is not a school activity. The teacher can just show up and enjoy it.
3. Organize all the logistics. Parents will need to use their own cars for transportation. Set a time to meet

at the school parking lot or at the field trip site. Make all the arrangements for the event.

4. Send a letter to all the parents explaining the outing. Here is a sample:

Since Mrs. Smith's class is studying the California Gold Rush, on October 12 we are going to visit the gold mine museum at Julian, where you can actually go down a mine shaft. We would like you to join us for this nonschool-sponsored activity. Mrs. Smith will be joining us as our guest. Here's how you can be a part of it. . . .

5. Invite the teacher, and let her simply enjoy a day with the families of her pupils. Even if only a few parents participate, you can have fun and get to know the teacher better.

We have discussed many aspects of establishing a relationship, promoting successful teacher conferences, and actively co-teaching with a positive teacher. But what if your child has a problem teacher?

What to Do About a Problem Teacher

At some point in your child's education you may have a personality conflict with a teacher. What can you do then?

Meet with the teacher, and express your concerns in a gracious and tactful way. As I mentioned earlier, use "I" statements rather than "you" statements as you talk about the problem. Instead of saying, "You are causing Sally to hate school," say, "I sense that Sally doesn't like coming to school anymore." Solicit suggestions from the teacher on what may be causing Sally's problem, and discuss various solutions. That conveys that you are not attacking the teacher but are seeking her advice on how to solve this problem. It is also important that you help the teacher understand why your child is upset by something that is going on in the class. If the teacher suggests that your child needs to change in some way and it seems reasonable, acknowledge it. Then tactfully ask how the teacher will change in order to create a win-win situation. Guide the conversation and suggestions to a satisfactory conclusion. If you can't resolve the problem with the teacher, it will be necessary to meet with the principal.

Meeting with the Principal

Visit the principal to discuss your concerns. However, realize that the principal will not outwardly agree with your criticism of the teacher. It is important that the principal maintain a positive and supportive relationship with all the teachers in the school. He will not undermine that relationship by siding against one of his staff, at least not in front of a parent. Does that mean the administrator is indifferent to your concern? Not at all. But he is not going to appear to undermine the teacher's classroom authority. It would be unprofessional of him to criticize a member of his staff in a conversation with a parent.

When talking with the principal, be gracious and positive about finding a solution. List your concerns on a notepad to refresh your memory as you talk. Your conversation needs to focus on the problems that are causing a disruption of your child's education. Also list a few suggestions for how you think the problem can be resolved. The principal will discuss your concerns with the teacher and seek a resolution. However, there are occasions when the best course of action is to transfer your child to another class.

Asking for a Transfer

The principal can transfer your child if he thinks it is the best alternative. When talking to the principal, emphasize that you are not attacking the teacher's competency—you are concerned that your child isn't doing as well as he could because of the problems between the teacher and the student. Reassignment may not be easy for an administrator to do. He may be concerned about setting a precedent; he may have no room in other classes; he may be concerned that such a move would undermine staff morale.

It is important that you use your best "people skills" to persuade the administrator that moving your child is the right thing to do. The principal most likely will not transfer a student simply because the parent doesn't like the teacher or the teacher is unpopular with students. The principal will need to see legitimate academic or social concerns that warrant such an action.

He may also want to wait a little while for space to open up in another classroom. In most schools, there is a constant stream of students moving in and out of classes due to families moving in and out of the community. The principal will most likely wait for an opening for your child.

Sometimes the problem is not the teacher but a specific book the class is reading or a subject they are studying. In this case you don't need to transfer your child to another class, but you may want to remove him temporarily from the classroom.

Removing Your Child from a Lesson

If the problem is a particular book or curriculum that is being used by the teacher, you may wonder whether you should remove your child from the classroom. I suggest to parents that they should seek to remove their child from a program when they can no longer influence their child's learning. That means that either they cannot influence their partner—the teacher—to choose another educational strategy or they cannot sufficiently undo what the child is learning in class.

You don't need to remove your child from an activity if you can influence the teacher to choose a better alternative. The mother of an eighth-grader told me how she was able to influence her child's teacher to alter the lesson plan. That not only saved her from having to remove her child from the class, but it improved the lesson plan for the other children too. Her teacher announced she would be showing an R-rated movie *(Blade Runner)* as part of a science fiction unit. "I called her, expressed appreciation for her hard work, and told her I felt R-rated movies were not appropriate for the classroom. I suggested some positive alternatives. She considered my suggestions and changed the movie," the mother related to me.

To Remove or Not to Remove Your Child

I do not believe you should remove your child from the classroom every time you disagree with a reading selection or a part of a curriculum. That would cause too much disruption in your child's education. Knowing when to remove your child from a classroom activity is subjective. Only you will be able to gauge when your child should not participate. In many situations, you may be able to reach a compromise with the teacher, such as an alternate reading assignment. However, at times you may have to decide to remove your child temporarily from the class.

You need to consider the four factors listed below when deciding whether to remove your child from a classroom activity. Try to be as objective as possible when considering these factors. Trust your sense of what is right for your child while at the same time considering whether you may be overreacting. It is best not to rush into a decision to remove your child because it can cause a disruption in his education in other subjects as well as in his social community at school. Here are the factors to consider.

How Truly Bad Is the Activity?

Establishing an activity's suitability requires discernment and objectivity. A case could be made for claiming that almost every subject is being taught improperly. The teacher could be slanting the subject too much to one political viewpoint or emphasizing student self-reliance too much, causing you to fear she is promoting rebellion. He may encourage world interdependence just a shade more than you feel is patriotic. You have to weigh how truly wrong the teacher is and how important the perceived error is.

An upset mother once called me concerning what her daughter was being told to read in class. The book was on Indian spiritism. The mother had already gone to the superintendent of the school district and told him to have the book removed or she would see to his dismissal. To get a better perspective on the situation, I asked her three questions. First, in what course was the book used? Second, how old was her daughter? Third, had the mother read the book? To my astonishment she answered that the book was used in an elective course on mythology; her daughter was a senior in high school; and, no, the mother had never read the book, but she thought the cover looked spooky.

Obviously, she was overreacting. I explained that, since the daughter was certainly old enough, she could use the book as a teaching tool to discuss their family's religious faith with her daughter in comparison to Indian spiritism. I pointed out that the situation could actually be an opportunity from God to strengthen the girl's faith, not an invitation from Satan to abandon it.

On the other hand, some subjects, such as sexuality, are handled so poorly by teachers or counselors that it is not good to have any exposure to their ideas at a young and impressionable age. This is a subjective and difficult decision for parents. My advice is not to make it without complete information. If your child is young, be sure to verify what he tells you happened in class by talking directly with the teacher. If you confront the teacher based on what you think happened in the class, you may be embarrassed to find out that you are reacting to false information.

How Emphatically Is It Taught?

You need to measure how strongly the teacher pushes a particular value or philosophy. The book in the above illustration was not taught as the truth but as one culture's mythology. A good education will include the views of others. However, sometimes the teacher's opinion is taught as the only way to think when, in fact, it is seriously in conflict with your family's beliefs. That is when action might be taken.

How Long Will the Lesson Last?

Sometimes a subject that you object to is covered briefly, and its long-term effects are small or nonexistent. It is hard to believe that a two-week drug abuse course that uses nondirective decision-making techniques (a poor approach for young people) will wipe out the years of moral character development you have built in your child. However, if a value-neutral approach to decision-making is emphasized week after week for several months, you will need to take action.

What Demonstrated Effects
Is It Having on Your Child?

Do you see your child exhibiting behavior that concerns you as a result of the program in question? Does your child seem upset when he comes home from school? Is he withdrawn? Does he act out with defiance? Is he more aggressive? Is he lethargic toward homework? Has he changed his thinking about a subject that is a core value of your family? Try to list actual behaviors or actions that you think may be linked to a particular program. That will help determine whether a negative impact is being made.

Again, are there specifics you can point to, or are you being too sensitive to what you fear may happen? Your reaction will depend on the age of your child. Young children may be more influenced by a program than older, more independent, children. A teenager should be able to separate himself from the teacher's lesson and realize that the teacher is not always right. With your help, your child may actually demonstrate greater character and conviction of thought because his beliefs are being tested in the classroom. Only you can judge whether he is ready for this.

In order to answer these four questions accurately, I suggest you obtain a copy of the material in question. Be sure you have examined all the information related to the lesson before you make your decision.

Summary

The important thing to remember in achieving a great education for your child is that you are the primary teacher. You span the years that will see many teachers come and go. It is up to you to be the educational leader in developing the kind of relationship with each teacher that maximizes your child's education. So, firmly but gently, take charge.

An important part of taking charge of your child's education is understanding the values and customs of the school. Your child's school is actually a small community with its own culture. The next chapter will help you understand that culture and show you how to guide your child through it with confidence.

4
Understand the Culture

Parent Power Tool #2: Understand the
Culture of Your Child's School

Your Goal
*I know who to talk to about a particular issue. I am sensitive
to the personalities and politics in the system. I know how to
present myself. I understand the jargon, customs, and beliefs
of school personnel. I help my child understand the positive
and negative aspects of the school's beliefs.*

The school is to your child what a foreign country is to a
tourist—exciting, scary, interesting, or boring, and almost
always different from his home culture. Your child has spent
five or six years in the environment you establish within your
home. He is used to the rules you set, the values you uphold,
the expectations you outline, and the habits you implant in him.
At school, though some rules will be the same as yours, others
will be different. The values expressed at school (from teachers and from peers) may be quite different from yours. Expectations placed upon your child may be different too.

One factor in maximizing your child's education that you
may have overlooked until now is an understanding of how the
public school culture works. This chapter will show you how
to recognize your school's particular culture and how to use it
to your child's advantage. If you do not take time to understand
your school's culture but try to be active in your child's education, you become very frustrated. You will bump up against the
cultural differences at school and not know what to do. What
do I mean when I refer to the culture of your child's public
school? Let me explain.

The dictionary defines *culture* as the "socially transmitted
behavior patterns, arts, beliefs, institutions, and all other products of human work and thought typical of a population or
community at a given time." Similarly, a subculture is a smaller

group within the larger culture that is unified by certain functions unique to that community. Your local school represents a subculture within America's public school culture. Your school does not share all the elements of the national public school culture. For instance, while nationally public schools are suffering academically, your school may excel; or, while across the nation the public school culture has severely restricted religious expression on campus, your school may have a very open and tolerant climate.

Tourist or Tour Guide?

In many ways, your child's school is like a foreign country. It has its own language, customs, beliefs, government, and even food. (Remember your old school cafeteria?) You will need the same skills and tools to function in the school as you would in a forcign country: a map, a dictionary, and a knowledge of the culture. As a parent, you will interact with your school's culture as either a tourist or a tour guide. When you visit the school, how do you interact with the natives of that culture? What do you expect? What do you give? What do you receive?

The Tourist

Have you ever been to a foreign country and felt confused or frustrated in trying to communicate with the people there?

A tourist typically visits a foreign country to get something out of it for himself. For him, seeing the culture means viewing it through the tinted windows of an air-conditioned motor coach. He wants to see the points of interest the culture has to offer but expects to see them while still enjoying the amenities of his own culture.

"Why don't they speak English?" he asks. He is frustrated that the banks close for two hours in the middle of the day. He never does figure out the currency exchange rates. He'd rather eat a Big Mac for lunch than a slice of the local delicacy. He is interested in stopping somewhere long enough to take a picture so he can prove to his friends back home that he was actually there. He has no real investment in the culture. He understands little. He takes from it rather than giving to it.

Many public school parents are like tourists in the school culture. Lacking understanding of the culture, they are amazed that the lessons taught in their child's classroom are different from those taught around their dining table at home.

The tourist-parent, like the old hymn says, is "just a'passin' through." He does not care to understand the school. He makes no investment of his time. He is interested in what he gets from it rather than what he contributes to it.

The child of the tourist parent will get an education. It may be good, or it may be bad. Unfortunately, the parent will not know how it happened. He will not be able to effectively correct a problem created in the school, nor will he be able to build on the success fostered by the school. The learning process is a mystery to him. *I take my child to the bus stop each morning and pick him up each afternoon,* he thinks. *After a few years, my child is educated. That's what is important.*

If you are a tourist in your local school, your child will suffer. He needs your guidance and support. He is the real tourist. Each new classroom is like a new country for him. He needs someone who can help him understand the culture he is in. He needs a guide.

The Tour Guide

The tour guide helps the tourist survive and even enjoy the strange culture. The tour guide understands the language and the local customs. He could give a lecture on the history of the culture, its religion, and its politics. Sometimes he must intercede for the tourist in a tangle with the locals. Like the tourist, he may be a foreigner to the culture they are visiting. Yet he can function better than the tourist. He can stand with a foot in each culture. He is a friend to both the tourist and the native.

In this analogy, the tourist is the child and the tour guide, the parent. The child is the unacquainted visitor. The child, like a tourist in a foreign land, skips through the school in search of the new and the interesting. The child is interested in what he can receive from, not what he can give to, the school.

The parent is the tour guide who must watch over the child's activity, intercede for the child at times, and help the child appreciate other people's views while remaining confident about his own. The parent maintains a friendly and welcome relationship with the school personnel. He understands the politics, personalities, and assumptions of the school staff. He is adequately acquainted with the philosophy that undergirds the school's teaching and can interpret it for the child. Like the tourist who travels from country to country, the child moves each year to different classes, different teachers, and even different schools. At each stop the child needs a guide to make the journey an enriching one.

For instance, your teenage daughter may mention that her teacher endorses a particular political stance that you oppose. As a tour guide you can discuss with her the various views on the issue and explain why you hold a different position. You are helping her understand the teacher's view as well as helping her think through your family's position. That is an essential part of creating a positive public school experience. To be able to discuss such issues with your child you need to understand the values and methods of instruction in the school.

Tour Guide Training

Being a tour guide requires training. It requires that you make a special effort to understand the culture of your school and guide your child through it. You can train yourself by doing the following:

1. *Spend Time with Those in the Public School Culture.* Volunteer at school and in your child's class. Regularly communicate with the teacher.

   Bob is a parent who found that he learned a lot about how his son's school functioned by volunteering one morning each week in the nurse's office. It put him in regular contact with the school's administrators and secretaries. It also made him a welcome and appreciated face in the school. If he had a suggestion or concern, the school personnel listened favorably to him.

"My work schedule allows me to do this, and I find it is the best way to get the pulse of the school," he said.

2. *Read Books That Will Help You Understand the Culture.* For example, if the teacher is using a teaching method that is new to you, ask him for a book or article that explains more about it. If a new program is being used in your school, such as whole-language reading, ask for a range of materials, both pro and con, so you will understand its advantages and disadvantages.

When you are researching a subject, be sure to read material that will give you a balance. If you read an article that is critical of the method your child's teacher uses, try to find one that is supportive of it. You might even ask the teacher to explain the pros and cons of her method.

Once you understand what is being taught, or the method a teacher uses, you can guide your child through its positive and negative effects. You will know just how to support and maximize the positive things she is exposed to in the classroom, and you can teach her discernment or even counteract the negative.

For instance, the whole-language reading method is being used in many elementary classrooms to teach reading. To its credit, it emphasizes the fun of reading and exposes children to a wider variety of reading material than do most other methods. However, one of its weaknesses is its use of what it calls inventive spelling. The theory is that if the teacher corrects student spelling errors by marking their mistakes, the students will become discouraged and frustrated and will lose their enthusiasm for writing. Proponents of this method believe that students will grow into correct spelling as they read the words spelled correctly in other contexts. The problem is that many students never break bad spelling habits. If you understand this aspect of whole language, you can augment your child's education by teaching her correct spelling at home.

3. *Clearly Define Your Family's Culture.* By doing so, you can help your child function in both worlds with confidence. Think about your beliefs on academic, moral, philosophical, and spiritual issues. Write down the expectations you have for your child in both academic and social conduct. Write a family code of honor and review it with your child. The code of honor should include what you believe about such topics as honesty, trustworthiness, responsibility, punctuality, neatness, and hard work. With teenagers you can also discuss drugs, smoking, dating, and alcohol.

4. *Regularly Discuss the Differences and Similarities Between Your Family's Values and the Values of the School.* When you do this, your child will gain a greater sense of detachment and discernment regarding his life at school. He will see that values expressed in the classroom are not necessarily valid for him. He will be able to defend the reasons he holds to the family's convictions.

To discuss school issues with your child, you need to be familiar with the school. You need to have at least a basic understanding of the school's jargon and values.

The Jargon of the School

I thought about entitling this section, "Surviving in an Outcome-Based, Thematic, Whole Language, and Cooperative Learning School," to give an example of jargon—those mysterious terms unique to a certain group. Though public school teachers in the United States speak English, they have their own jargon: *educationese.* I made this point once during an interview on a radio station in the Midwest. During a commercial break the host exclaimed, "I never thought about it that way, but it sure is true. Just the other day, I had our state superintendent of education on this program and had to ask him to restate almost everything he said because I couldn't understand what he was talking about!" That radio host had encountered educationese—the language of the public school.

Words and phrases such as *restructuring, Bloom's taxonomy, critical thinking, journaling*, or *cooperative learning* are meaningless to you until you learn how your school's educators define them. Those words are used to describe subjects your children will learn or methods the teacher will be using. When you understand them, you are better able to explain them to your children and discuss them with the teacher.

If, for instance, the teacher tells you she is using "whole language" in the classroom, it may be meaningless to you. Yet it has important implications for your child's learning. Is it a good thing or a bad thing? Is it the right method for your child? How will "whole language" change how you help your child at home? Understanding what the teacher means when she uses a term will help you be more effective as you work with your child at home. You will know what the teacher is doing and why she is doing it.

The best way to understand the educational language of your child's school is to ask questions. When you hear a new term used during a parent-teacher conference, ask what it means. When you see a new term used in a school bulletin, ask about it. Four key questions to ask are:

1. What does the term mean?
2. How is it being applied in my child's school?
3. How does it improve my child's educational experience?
4. What are potential problems with the misapplication of this new concept? (Avoid appearing antagonistic with this question. Instead, ask it in a way that conveys to the teacher that you are eager to understand and curious about the education process.)

You can gain a lot of clarity about a term used at school from a little polite probing. Understanding your school's jargon will help you understand *what* and *how* your child is being taught. You may find things in your school you dislike, but you may not be able to change them. However, recognizing those things will help you understand the environment your child is in. That will enable you to better explain the positive and negative aspects of the lesson, book, or activity to your child.

Cultural Clashes

Your school officials and educators perceive certain things to be true about learning, values, children, parents, and what the school's role should be. It is important to understand the beliefs held by your child's teachers and school administrators. As a Christian, you will often have a different set of values from those taught in the public school. When a difference in values arises, you need to be equipped to do one of two things: 1) intercede for your child and ask the teacher to respect your values; 2) use the difference in values to teach your child discernment.

For instance, Jill is a mother whose high school son came home talking about the advantages of euthanasia—the act of causing a painless death to end suffering. That day at school his social studies teacher had started a discussion on assisted suicide. The teacher presented a one-sided view heavily favoring euthanasia. He even went so far as to ask the students to talk with their parents about writing a living will. Jill and her husband believe in the sanctity of life and that any form of assisted suicide or mercy killing is wrong. They used the bias of the teacher as an opportunity to discuss their beliefs and what the Bible says about the value of life with their son.

"We talk about our family's values all the time with our kids," Jill told me. "The next thing we're working on is the evolution issue. Our son and his father recently attended a seminar on creationism to help him have a better perspective on his beliefs as he goes through his biology class."

One of your greatest tools in creating a positive school experience for your children is to maintain an ongoing dialogue with them about your family's values. That will help your children hold to your values with greater confidence. You may also find that when your family talks openly and regularly about values your children will more readily come to you when they have a question or are challenged at school.

Your child's school will exhibit some type of value on many subjects. These values are an integral part of the culture of the school. When you understand what they are, you will be able to more effectively explain the positive and negative aspects of each one for your child. Later in this chapter, I will explain how to talk to the teacher and principal about your concerns with a subject.

But first, let's look at some brief descriptions of some of the more controversial issues you may encounter at school. I have also listed a few things to look for that are cause for concern, as well as what you can do immediately to help your child regarding each issue.

Multiculturalism

Two prominent views dominate this hotly debated subject. One rapidly emerging view is that the defining experience for each American is his or her ethnicity. Racial origin becomes paramount in understanding who an individual is and how he or she should live. Schools emphasizing this view highlight and celebrate preservation of past ethnic and cultural distinctions. On the other hand, there are those educators who see ethnicity as an enriching ingredient within the uniqueness of American culture, not separate from it. These educators see the American experience as formed by immigrants who cast off their old cultures and contributed to the formation of a new national identity. These teachers emphasize commonality of values based on modern Western civilization, rather than division of values based on cultural ancestry.

What to look for that should cause concern:

1. Watch carefully how your school teaches multiculturalism to see if there is a reasonable balance of views. Pay special attention to your child's social studies lessons.
2. Does the school seem to teach more about American's differences than it teaches about their similarities?
3. Does the teacher or school fail to give your child a firm grounding in the history and value of Western civilization?

How to talk to your child if you are concerned about multiculturalism at school:

1. Talk to your child about the beliefs that can bind Americans together such as freedom, the work ethic, capitalism, compassion, and democracy.
2. Discuss issues of race and cultural diversity in America with your child. During family devotions, incorporate lessons of racial equality and respect. These could include the fact that God "shows no partiality" (Acts 10:34) and that in His eyes "there is neither Jew nor Greek, there is neither slave nor free man, there is neither male nor female" (Gal. 3:28).

Global Education

Global education is a movement within public education that seeks to create loyalty among students to a world society. There is an increasing trend toward global awareness in classrooms. Some schools emphasize international understanding to such an extent that patriotism and the value of American citizenship are diminished. However, many schools use the term *global education* to mean only an expanded instruction in world geography, cultures, and politics.

What to look for that should cause concern:

1. Examine how the teacher approaches teaching about the world. Does he emphasize "world citizenship" to the exclusion of American citizenship? Does the school lack an appropriate balance of global awareness and patriotism?
2. Does the teacher tend to emphasize the mistakes and abuses of American foreign policy or American businesses in other countries without a balanced presentation of the good that has been done?

How to talk to your child about global education:

1. Teach your child about America's heritage. Read and discuss books about the Founding Fathers.
2. Use patriotic holidays such as Independence Day, Veterans Day, and Presidents' Day to help your child understand what it means to be an American.
3. Discuss with your child examples of how American international trade and capitalism have brought prosperity and opportunity around the world. You can often find good examples in magazines and newspapers.

Self-Esteem Courses

Does your school use a self-esteem program, and if so, what kind? Too often programs used to lift self-esteem employ only gimmicks and games with little actual benefit. Many Christian parents are understandably concerned that self-esteem programs will create self-centeredness in a child. They are also concerned that in trying to promote self-reliance these programs will turn a child's heart away from depending on the Lord.

Programs that emphasize introspection and the sharing of feelings have not proven as successful in boosting self-esteem as those programs that focus on student achievement and skills development. The approach your school takes to develop student self-esteem will set a definite tone within the school.

What to look for that should cause concern:

1. Your school may have a separate program to teach self-esteem. If it does, carefully examine it to see how it teaches self-esteem. (Chapter 5 will provide greater detail on how to know a good program from a poor one.)
2. The teacher lowers academic standards with the reasoning that she wants to boost student self-esteem.
3. Is there often more social time than academic time in the class?
4. The school or teacher gives out awards for things that require little or no effort by the students.

How to talk to your child about a self-esteem program:

1. Regularly give your child sincere affirmation about his or her behavior that demonstrates good character, attitudes, and abilities. (More on this in chapter 5.)
2. Maintain high yet reasonable academic expectations for your child.
3. Be sure your child is progressing well in developing academic skills. He doesn't need to be getting all "As" to have a healthy self-esteem, but he does need to be seeing success and progress.
4. Teach your child a biblical view of self-image based upon God's unconditional love for us. That is a sure foundation for striking a balance between self-worth and humility.

Character Education

Allen Elementary School has it tough. Almost 60 percent of the students come from single-parent homes, and 78 percent of the student body are in families that receive Aid to Families with Dependent Children. The classroom environment used to be plagued with discipline problems. Only 10 percent of students' homework assignments were completed and turned in to the teachers.

In 1989, the new principal, Rudolfo Bernardo, started a character education program to change student attitudes about school, learning, and themselves. Under Bernardo's leadership, teachers developed a list of thirty-six values that, if adopted by the students, would improve their behavior and attitudes. Today, the values are taught using three steps: each Monday, Bernardo announces and explains the Word of the Week, which is the value that the teachers will emphasize each day; Tuesday, Wednesday, and Thursday each teacher gives a ten-minute lesson with plenty of illustrations reinforcing the importance of that week's value; finally, on Friday, the students gather for an assembly, and one class performs a skit that demonstrates the value in action.

The results have been nothing short of phenomenal. The number of students suspended went from 150 in the 1989–90 school year to only ten the following year. Student scores on the California Achievement Test (a test used by many states) jumped 50 percent in just three years. The school's overall academic standing went from twenty-eighth out of Dayton's thirty-three elementary schools to fifth. There is now a waiting list of parents who want to enroll their children in Allen Elementary School.

It is important for you to understand that a school's values don't just happen; they are a direct result of what the school's leadership does or neglects to do. Unfortunately, many schools have no character education plan.

What to look for that should cause concern:

1. The school has no written commitment or plan to teach good character to students.
2. If there is a plan, it is not implemented consistently.
3. The school maintains a "value-neutral" stance when teaching decision making.
4. Courses on drugs, alcohol, and sexual conduct tend to be nonjudgmental.
5. The teacher does not maintain a well-disciplined and respectful climate in the classroom.

How to talk to your child regarding character education:

1. Develop a "family code of honor" concerning character expectations. Regularly discuss it with your child.
2. Model good character for your child.
3. Maintain a balance of love and limits for your child.
4. Point out to your child examples of the rewards and consequences for good and bad character in society.
5. Spend time in family Bible devotions discussing the spiritual basis for good character qualities.

Sex Education

Sex education courses have changed a lot in recent years. Too many teachers today expect that students will have sex and are not surprised when they live down to their expectations. The lessons have become much more explicit than most Christian parents want. In Georgia, for instance, a state advisory panel recently recommended that the definition of "family" be changed to include couples who live together out of wedlock, whether they are heterosexuals or homosexuals. They also proposed that sixth-graders learn about condoms. An outcry from conservative parents forced a compromise in that state.

Sex education isn't just a subject for secondary schools anymore. There is a growing trend among sex education organizations to push for sex education to begin as early as kindergarten. It is very natural for you to be concerned about an educator teaching your child about sex when it is such an intimate and value-laden subject.

What to look for that should cause concern:

1. The school starts teaching sexually-oriented lessons, other than about hygiene, in elementary grades.
2. The sex education course teaches students how to use contraceptives.

3. The sex education course does not emphasize abstinence to students and does not expect them to
   abstain.
4. The "family life" course defines family other than
   people related by blood, marriage, or adoption.
5. The sex education course goes beyond the biology of
   reproduction and spends most of its time on a range of
   sexuality issues (i.e., lifestyles, stereotypes, gender
   politics).

How to talk to your child about sex education:

1. When you feel the time is right, read an age-appro-
   priate, Christian book on sex and discuss it with your
   child.
2. Help your child see the beauty of the marriage relationship.
3. Center your family devotions around such themes as
   marriage, abstinence, and procreation.
4. Teach your teenager how to develop a dating life that
   is respectful of the opposite sex.
5. Help your child learn to discern between love and
   infatuation. An excellent resource on this is Ray
   Short's book, *Sex, Love, or Infatuation: How Can I
   Really Know?*

Religious Holidays

Holidays are often the focus of cultural clashes between
Christian parents and school officials. Even many Christian
teachers who have strong religious convictions do not teach
about Christmas or Easter because the culture of the school
will not allow it. That occurs not because the law demands
it—and sometimes not even because the school demands
it—but because the teachers assume they can't. I recently
received a letter from a teacher who explained that for the last
ten years she had not taught about the birth of Christ at
Christmas. The school hadn't officially restricted her; she just
assumed it was improper.

In many schools, the staff acknowledges Christmas and Easter only as secular holidays, yet they celebrate Halloween with pictures of witches, ghosts, and little devils. Their double standard about acknowledging religion never occurs to them.

That is not to say that all schools ban holiday celebrations. Your school may be like many that have Christmas concerts, sing Christmas carols, and teach the religious history of the holiday. Such schools still exist—with the law on their side, by the way—and you may be fortunate enough to have your child in one.

What to look for that should cause concern:

1. Your school district has a written policy severely restricting holiday celebrations, such as banning references to Christmas and forbidding students to sing religious Christmas carols.
2. Your school spends weeks preparing for Halloween with stories about witches, ghosts, demons, and the dead.
3. The religious nature of holidays is not taught at all.

How to talk to your child when holidays are a problem at school:

1. Be sure to teach your child at home about the history and meaning of each holiday.
2. If your child is old enough to understand, use the restrictions on holidays in the school as an object lesson to illustrate how non-Christians don't understand the importance of biblical truths (such as the birth, death, and resurrection of Christ).

Outcome-Based Education (OBE)

Judging from the telephone calls I receive, the biggest concern of parents right now is a new approach schools are implementing called *outcome-based education*. "What's all the fuss about holding schools accountable for outcomes?" you may ask. Isn't that what schools are supposed to do—produce measurable results in student academic achievement? Although OBE does attempt to do this, it also creates a number of new problems. Because OBE has the potential to greatly alter your child's school, I will explain this issue a little more fully.

Proponents of OBE point out that, in the past, reform efforts have focused primarily on inputs rather than outcomes. That is, reformers have concerned themselves with such things as more time spent on homework, more time spent on academic subjects, and more up-to-date books. The idea was that if all the parts were input properly the outcome would automatically be quality. More recently many reformers have shifted their primary concerns to the ends—demonstrable results—of education rather than merely the processes.

But OBE goes further than that. It seeks to change the mission and structure of schooling as well. For instance, instead of asking of an English program, "What should a graduate know about literature?" OBE reformers want schools to ask broader questions such as, "What will demonstrate good thinking skills about written material?" William Spady, a leading proponent of OBE, calls this "role performance" because it demonstrates knowledge and skills that are useful in roles outside of school. The problem is that when schools set goals around broader life skills, high academic standards may suffer.

For instance, in the example above, schools might replace classic literature with watered-down juvenile books as long as thinking skills about written material are demonstrated. That is all the more possible because OBE strongly advocates the idea that no students will fail since they will be taught over and over until the desired outcome is reached. Since these outcomes must fit all students—both high and low achievers—critics rightly fear that schools will create average rather than excellent standards. Defining, for example, that students will be problem solvers does not guarantee that rigorous math teaching will occur.

Critics are also concerned that OBE schools are not just including academic outcomes but emotional and social outcomes in their agenda as well. Since OBE seeks to define lifelong skills rather than merely academic skills, there is a real danger that many outcomes will coerce proper values such as tolerance, self-esteem, and environmental sensitivity. There is a difference between teaching about a value and making the adoption and demonstration of that value an outcome to be graded. For instance, "All students will value democracy" is coercing a value whereas "All students will understand democracy" is not. As a teacher I may want students to value democracy and even teach to that end, but to grade them on how much they demonstrate appreciation for it is inappropriate.

Probing Questions to Ask School Officials

Here are a few questions you might ask your child's teacher, principal, superintendent, or school board concerning OBE and your child. Asking the questions in a spirit of healthy dialogue rather than debate may prove enlightening to educators and may cause them to think critically before jumping onto the OBE bandwagon.

1. What specifically will the district do differently to encourage all students to excel in the basic skills of reading, writing, and computation?
2. What has the district done to accommodate varying levels of learning ability and motivation? After all, not all students are destined to perform in roles as rocket scientists or surgeons.
3. Do the district outcomes represent high levels of academic performance, or are they generalized life skills that can be met without rigorous and challenging academic expectations?
4. OBE uses a variety of existing instructional methods such as whole language/thematic curriculum and co-operative learning. Why will these existing inputs produce better outcomes under OBE than they have in the past?
5. Has the school distinguished between establishing performance outcomes on academic subjects and dictating proper values?

How to help your child in an OBE school:

1. Meet with your child's teacher, and ask what all the changes will mean for your child. Take notes, and ask for definitions or explanations of new terms the teacher may use.
2. Ask for a list of classroom learning expectations. Specifically what will your child be expected to know and do by the end of the year?
3. Regularly talk to your child regarding his progress and his classroom activities. This will help you determine if the school's theory of instruction is being properly applied by the teacher.
4. If you believe your child is not being challenged enough, ask the teacher to provide him with more rigorous material.
5. If the teacher is teaching a value contrary to what you want your child to learn, ask the teacher to provide an alternative program, a more balanced view, or that your child be excused from the lesson.

For most of this section on "Culture Clashes," I have emphasized how to talk to your child about an issue of concern at school. You will notice that in the section on OBE I gave you questions to ask school officials and the teacher. That is because OBE has to do with the entire structure of the school program, not a specific lesson. On any one of these issues, however, you may find that you need to talk to the teacher or principal about your concerns. There are three techniques for successfully approaching the "natives" of the public school culture.

Three Techniques for Negotiating with the "Natives"

Like any traveler in a foreign culture, you need to know how to negotiate with the natives. In your local school, that means knowing how to get what you want for your child from school personnel. Here are three proven techniques.

Technique #1: Your Class, My Child

This is a nonthreatening way to approach the teacher when you do not want your child participating in a particular classroom activity. Start your conversation with the teacher by acknowledging—with genuine respect—her authority to teach her subject as she sees fit. This will circumvent the natural defensiveness any teacher is bound to feel when confronted by a disapproving parent. No one likes to be criticized. When you complain about the teacher's selection of materials or teaching methods, she may receive it as nothing more than criticism. By acknowledging her authority, you put her at ease.

Follow this with a friendly but firm reminder that though the classroom is hers, the child is yours. You know how you want him to develop, and long after he has graduated from this class you will still be responsible for his academic and moral growth. Therefore, without challenging the teacher's right to teach, you are asking her to provide an alternative educational activity for your child. That does not mean having him sit in the hall while the lesson is taught. An alternative educational activity means he works quietly at his desk on another assignment or goes to the library. If the objectionable activity will only last one day you may want to give your child an excused absence and plan a fun activity together for that day. If communicated in a friendly manner, most teachers will honor your request.

Wanda is a mother who called me because of her concern about a book her son's class was reading. She felt the story—about a rebellious boy—placed parents in a negative light. She called the teacher and told her that she would like to chat for a few minutes after school. When they met, Wanda began by telling her how much her son, Timothy, enjoyed the class. They talked for a few minutes about the previous week's lesson on Mexico, and Wanda told the teacher how much fun she had had with Timothy preparing a platter of enchiladas for the class party at the end of the week-long unit.

Then Wanda said, "You're a wonderful teacher, and I appreciate what you're doing for my son. Something's come up, however, that I feel uncomfortable about, and I thought I should tell you about it." She went on to explain her thoughts about the book. The teacher explained why she chose the book for the class to read and that she didn't see a problem with using it.

"I understand your point, and I respect your right to choose that book," Wanda responded, "But I'd feel more comfortable if Timothy could read another book during that time. Could that be done without a lot of disruption of your lesson?"

"Certainly," said the teacher, and she took the mother to a bookshelf in the classroom full of children's books. "Feel free to select a book you'd like Timothy to read."

This technique works well when you are trying to have your child "opted out" of a specific lesson or activity. If you want to influence the teacher to change something she is doing with the entire class, you have to persuade her that your concerns are valid enough for her to adopt as well. Technique number two can help you do that.

Technique #2: Help Me Understand (and I'll Help You Understand)

This is another nonthreatening approach. Ask the teacher to help you understand the reason behind a method she is using or an activity she is having the class do. As you discuss the issue, you can guide the conversation to address your concerns. You do not need to declare that you are going to help her understand your concern. Instead, simply bring it up by way of exploring her explanation of the issue.

After I explained this technique to a mother living in New Mexico, she used it successfully to resolve her concern regarding a daily classroom practice. The teacher was having the children recite a pledge to Mother Earth along with their normal flag salute. The mother was concerned about the activity for two reasons. First, it trivialized the importance of the Pledge of Allegiance to the American flag. Second, it personified the earth as if it could appreciate the child's allegiance. The mother was concerned that the activity was too close to spiritualizing nature.

The mother wanted to see the classroom activity changed not only because she felt it was inappropriate but because the pledge was recited every day. Having her child sit out every day would have been awkward. She visited the teacher and used the help-me-understand technique. Through her friendly, conversational manner she found out that the teacher merely wanted the students to avoid littering and to be aware of what they could do to keep their community clean. She had seen the earth pledge written somewhere and thought it sounded good. In the course of the conversation, the mother explained her concerns, and the teacher agreed that students could get confused by the pledge. The teacher decided to change the pledge to a simple promise about littering and environmental awareness.

There are occasions when talking to the teacher doesn't solve the problem. You should always start with the teacher, but if you are not satisfied with the teacher's response, you should visit the school principal.

Technique #3: I Thought I Should Alert You to a Potentially Embarrassing Situation

This is one way to approach your school's principal. She is used to hearing parental complaints. If you approach her as just another complainer, you run the risk of being categorized as a "problem parent."

If, however, you come to her as a friend and supporter of the school, someone who is protective of the school's reputation, her response may be quite different. This technique brings to the administrator's awareness something she might not have known was going on.

After I explained this technique to a mother from North Carolina, she used it to protect not only her child but also the entire school from a bad program. She contacted our office, concerned because her daughter was listening to self-hypnosis audiotapes in class and learning how to meditate. The guidance counselor was coming into class once a week and leading the children through guided imagery exercises.

The mother found hypnotic tapes in the local library that were explicitly labeled as New Age. She took those tapes, along with a tape that was being used in her daughter's class, to the principal. She started the conversation saying, "I thought I should alert you to a potentially embarrassing situation." He was all ears. She played the New Age audiotape and then played the tape used in the classroom. He listened for a few minutes and, after recognizing the similarity, immediately called the district superintendent. Together they decided to meet with the guidance counselor and stop her activity in the entire school. They also found out she had been using two other activities steeped in New Age philosophy and ordered her to discontinue those as well. The principal thanked the mother for helping him stop a program that he feared would have been an embarrassment to the school if it had been made public.

Your learning the lines of authority in the school is very important for your child's education. You need to know whom to go to with your concerns. The traditional line of authority begins with your child's teacher. Try your best to find a solution to your concern with the teacher. If you cannot do that, go to the principal. You may also want to bring a friend or your spouse along. You will feel less intimidated, and if you get flustered, your partner can help you express your concern. Avoid the appearance of going over the head of the teacher or the principal. Instead, try asking, "Who else can help us with this issue?" Solicit advice. In extreme cases you may need to visit the school district superintendent for counsel on how to resolve a problem.

Let's look at some examples of mothers interceding for their children and changing the curriculum. One evening at church, Melanie's family watched a Christian video explaining the New Age movement. Afterward, her third-grade daughter, Holly, said, "We do that at school," referring to the meditation shown in the video.

Melanie spoke with several other mothers whose children attended the same school. Their children reported being involved in yoga and guided imagery in their class. They discovered that it was a teacher's aide, not the teachers, who was leading children in this program. Melanie went to her child's teacher and voiced her concerns while also letting her know she was not attacking the teacher. As a courtesy to the teacher, she let her know she was going to also speak with the principal.

Eight parents visited the principal and calmly discussed why they disagreed with the activity and did not want it taught to their children. Melanie believed that having eight parents visit the principal caused him to sit up and take notice. One parent had contacted him previously and received no positive response. This time, however, he set up a meeting with the teacher's aide, the parents, a representative group of teachers, the superintendent, a school board member, and himself. They discussed the issue again with the principal acting as moderator. "The teachers seemed to be defending their colleague rather than the curriculum," Melanie told me later. "But," she continued, "the administrators and school board member seemed very open to our concerns. They also liked the way we conducted ourselves in the whole matter. We didn't come in blasting the school."

Soon after the meeting, the principal decided to eliminate the curriculum from the school. "In hindsight," said Melanie, "we think two factors influenced the principal's decision. First, he didn't want to split the community over the issue. Seeing eight concerned parents in his office really impressed him. Second, we prayed a lot. That definitely turned the tide. We feel God opened the principal's heart to what we were saying in the meeting."

The first step in using your school's culture to maximize your child's education is to recognize that the culture does exist. Your school's educators have a unique way of doing things based partly on their assumptions about education and partly on their personalities. Someone once said that an organization is a direct reflection of the person at the top. Your child's classroom is organized around the personality and beliefs of the teacher. Your child's school is organized around the personality and beliefs of the principal. Now that you recognize the impact of your school's culture, you need to think about how you will guide your child through it.

Summary

You need to recognize that your child's school has its own culture which may have values similar to those of your home, as well as some that are very different from yours. Its culture is made up of the language educators use, the traditions and practices they have, and the values or beliefs they express.

The way you interact with the school's culture falls into one of two categories: tourist or tour guide. Your child is the tourist in the foreign culture of the school. Your goal should be to act as a tour guide for your child. That involves learning about the school's culture and being able to explain it to your child. It means knowing how to communicate with the natives and interceding for your child's benefit when necessary.

When you use the techniques outlined in this chapter, you will gain greater control over what your child learns, and you can be confident that your child will develop well.

The next chapter shows you how to guide your child to develop good character qualities and attitudes. This is important because in any school environment there are plenty of temptations from peers to do the wrong thing.

5
Build Character

Parent Power Tool #3:
Encourage Your Child at Home

Your Goal
I look for opportunities to make affirming statements about my child's abilities, attitudes, or character. I give my child lots of encouragement throughout each week. I have reasonable yet high expectations of my child and hold him or her to those expectations.

Giving gifts can be expensive. How would you like to be able to give one of the best gifts in the world to your children? This chapter will show you exactly how to do that. Not only is this gift one of the most precious things you can give, it will last a lifetime! And best of all, it will cost you absolutely nothing, and you can give it every day. I'm referring to the gift of encouragement.

Many people feel so awkward about giving an encouraging word to someone else that they seldom do it. This wonderful family-building tool often gets neglected. Yet, it is one of the most essential tools you can use in creating a strong family and helping your child in school. Encouraging your child is a skill you can learn.

Encouragement is unique in that it becomes its own power generator. Once you have planted an encouraging word it goes to work. It travels throughout the other person's memory, repeating your words over and over. Encouragement creates pleasant thoughts in the recipient's mind. It creates energy within the person and helps him perform better than he thought he could. An encouraging word will continue to cycle within the person's thoughts, creating new power for pressing forward with his efforts and goals.

Being an encourager also has its benefits. You become a much more positive person. An encourager looks for things to affirm in other people. When that becomes a habit, you will find that you are focusing on the good qualities of other people rather than their faults. When you learn to be a consistent and frequent encourager, life becomes brighter and you become more optimistic.

Another benefit to you, the encourager, is that people like being around you. We all know someone who is the sourpuss, the pessimist, who sees everyone's faults. I do not like being around negative people, and I'll bet you don't either. When you become an active encourager, people will gravitate toward you. They will enjoy their contact with you because they sense that you appreciate them. Being encouraged is such a pleasurable experience, the people receiving the encouragement will come back for more. They may not even know why they like hanging around you so much. All they know is that they feel great whenever you are near.

A third benefit of being an encourager is that you will create greater intimacy and bonding with your children. Intimacy encompasses sharing something deep inside you. Being intimate means being open with someone and creating deep familiarity with that person. The act of encouragement means you are looking inside the heart of your children and making affirming statements about who they are as well as what they do. This will create a new level of communication between you. We all need someone who believes in us, who sees our best, and who cheers us in our lives. When you do this with your children, they will feel more secure in sharing their fears, hurts, and failures with you. They will trust their fragile feelings with you more readily because you have repeatedly demonstrated your belief and confidence in them.

Nathanial Hawthorne, the famous American author of the nineteenth century, owed his success to the encouragement of his wife, Sophia. The story is told that before he was a writer, he worked in a customhouse. One day he lost his job. He went home a broken man to tell his wife that he was a failure. However, Sophia greeted the news with joy. "Now you can write your book!" she exclaimed.

"And what will we live on while I'm writing it?" he asked. She took him to the bedroom and opened a drawer full of cash.

"Where on earth did you get that?" he asked in astonishment.

"I've always known you were a man of genius," she answered. "I knew that someday you would write an immortal masterpiece. So every week, out of money you have given me for housekeeping, I have saved something. We now have enough to last us one whole year."

Hawthorne proceeded to write one of the most recognized novels in American history, *The Scarlet Letter*.

Encouragement says, "I believe in you." It recognizes in others what they often do not see in themselves. As the very word implies, it empowers a person to take courage over seemingly insurmountable circumstances. Encouragement can do this because words have power.

The Power of Words

Think for a moment of something positive someone said to you in years gone by. Maybe it was a comment that seemed insignificant at the time, yet you remember it to this day. I remember a man once telling me when I was thirteen that he was impressed that I looked him in the eye while conversing. I'm sure he forgot about his comment before he got home for dinner that night. Yet I remember his words and have often thought about them while carrying on a conversation these many years later.

Words are the most powerful things in the world. With words, wars are started. For words, men will lay down their lives. Words can negotiate peace. Words can seal multi-million dollar deals or cause the stock market to plummet. They can make us laugh, and they can move us to tears. Words can draw a family together, or words can drive son from father and daughter from mother. There is nothing so full of uplifting potential in all the earth as words. Yet for all their power, we use words daily with only the slightest awareness of their impact.

God gave us language as a unique gift among His creatures. Because of their power, words are sacred—worthy of great respect and singularly used for doing good. Much good can be done with few words. The Lord's Prayer contains only 66 words; the Gettysburg Address, 269; the Ten Commandments use 298.

The spoken or written word is active. It has the power to create entirely new realities in our minds. Read a good novel, and you can be transported to another time or place. The characters in the story are fictional, yet when we read about them, we can become so engrossed in the story that their reality can overshadow our own. We worry about the characters. We laugh when they are happy and cry when they are in pain. We are moved to a variety of emotions for people that do not exist! That is the power of words.

Vitamins for Life

The spoken word can be like a vitamin or a virus. Once uttered it travels through the ear and lodges in the brain. Once in our memory it is difficult to remove. It attaches itself to our emotions, our self-confidence, our goals, and our habits. Words can be so powerful that one little sentence can completely change the way we think for years to come. "You will never amount to anything!" is one type of ugly virus that attacks a person's motivation or sense of self. It can create physical sickness in a person. It is capable of scarring a person for life.

There are antidotes, however, for virus words. The antidotes are vitamin words. Many parents give their children vitamins every day to improve their health and ward off illness. You can give your children words for their emotional health every day as well. Your children's minds can be so filled with words that give them confidence and healthy self-esteem that they will have the emotional tools to fight off the virus words they encounter.

Vitamin A—Assure. Each day you can assure your child that he or she is good or capable or normal or beautiful.

Vitamin B—Believe. Look for opportunities to send to your child's mind strong I-know-you-can-do-it statements.

Vitamin C—Comfort. When your child is hurt or sad, you can inject a strong dose of comforting words.

Vitamin D—Develop. Help your child with words that develop his talents and abilities.

Vitamin E—Expect. When you have reasonable, yet high, expectations for your child, you convey that you see in her the capability to reach them.

How to Encourage Your Child

By now you should have a good idea of the importance of encouragement. Let's look at what encouragement means. At the root of the word is *courage*, meaning strength of heart (*cor* is Latin for heart). With courage you can overcome adversity. That does not mean you have no fear, it means you overcome your fear by drawing on an inner strength. It is an attitude of confidence and optimism deep inside you. It sees the dark ahead but feels a light inside. It knows that life is tough but that you are tougher. To encourage your child means to infuse your child with inner strength. When you encourage your child, you are helping him to live in courage.

To learn how to encourage your child, you must first look at what discourages him. The thing that will most discourage your child in school, at home, or on the sports field is a singular focus on results without also acknowledging effort.

How he views his achievement leads to how he views himself. Is he clumsy? Does he drop the baseball too many times? Does he seldom complete his homework? Does he find his math class confusing? When he repeatedly perceives that he cannot achieve, he can spiral into a cycle of discouragement that eats away at his sense of self. He may move from telling himself "I don't understand how to do it" to "I'm stupid." He moves from a statement about his achievement to a declaration about his character. "I have failed" becomes "I am a failure."

Focusing on the effort to achieve is an essential component to encouraging your child. Too often a student focuses on only one achievement standard—the grade—as a sign of her worth. Because of that singular focus, she misses the many positive demonstrations of who she is, in the process of, for instance, doing her homework assignment. In order to complete her homework, she must demonstrate several character qualities. She must be *responsible* enough to remind herself of what the assignment is. She must be *organized* enough to set aside time to work on it and create a plan of attack for completing it. She must be *disciplined* enough to work on it. She must be *conscientious* enough to write it neatly. She must be *diligent* enough to complete it on time. She demonstrates five character qualities in the process of doing her homework.

The grade is an important indicator of certain types of achievement, and it is helpful for opening up opportunities as your child goes into higher grade levels. But what really counts in life is the development of your child's habits, character, and attitude. A gifted student may easily make good grades with little effort. If the grade is the primary focus of your attention, he will not develop the character necessary for true success in life.

The effort to do his best and make steady progress is an important factor in developing your child's confidence and character. How he conducts himself in the process of achieving is as important to his development as the achievement itself.

Conduct is the barometer of character. Poor conduct indicates a lack of inner character. Good conduct indicates good character qualities. The key to encouraging your child toward the formation of good habits, good character, and good attitudes is to move beyond the final result and focus on the character he exhibits in his effort to achieve.

For example, perhaps one day your child goes to her room after school and works diligently on her homework without your having to remind her. Immediately success bells begin ringing! Her behavior is just what you have hoped for. But what is most important is the character and attitude her action demonstrates. Her behavior demonstrates responsibility, diligence, initiative, hard work, and independence. It is those character qualities and attitudes that you want to strengthen and make habitual in her life. The technical skills and knowledge are secondary to the life-impacting habits of character she is developing. Furthermore, the technical skills and knowledge—the subject of her learning—will come easier as she develops those habits of character.

Catch 'Em Being Good

There is a simple two-step process for encouraging good character and good attitudes in your child. Although it is simple, it is often overlooked and will require some practice on your part.

The two-step process is this:

1. Recognize the conduct.
2. Reveal the character or attitude it demonstrated.

Fortunately, encouraging your child can be done at any time. You don't have to pour on the encouraging words immediately after he has done something. If you forgot to make an encouraging comment after he completed his homework the other night, you can refer to it now. The encouragement will still have impact. When you acknowledge the behavior to your child, you are letting him know exactly what he did that was good. But, using the power of words, move beyond the behavior to reveal to your child the character or attitude his behavior exhibited.

If your child turns in his homework on time, you can recognize that and then reveal his character of responsibility or punctuality or hard work. You might say, "I'm glad that you turned your assignment in on time. I'm proud that you stick with a project until it is completed."

As you encourage character, be flexible. The same behavior in your child can reveal several different character qualities or attitudes. For example, Tammy decided to redo her homework and make it neater. That demonstrated hard work, neatness, responsibility, and patience. It would be best for her parents to select one of those qualities to emphasize. In this instance, Tammy's dad may want her to see the value of patience. He says, "It's great that you cleaned up your rough draft and made your homework so neat. I'm impressed with your patience."

Too often parents and teachers take a student's good behavior for granted and only his bad behavior is highlighted. After all, he is supposed to turn in his assignments, he is supposed to listen carefully in class, he is supposed to be responsible. Only when he is not doing these things do we make a comment.

When you become an encourager, you reverse that habit in your own life and begin to catch your child being good. You look for opportunities to point out when he is, for instance, responsible and how proud you are of him—even if it was the only high point of his behavior that day. You make sure he understands that you noticed his helpfulness or patience or generosity.

You can target your encouraging words to specific character qualities that will help your child learn at school. Your words can give him the foundation for greater success in the classroom each day.

Encouragement as a Teacher

Ignorance and incompetence are the enemies of learning and personal development. The world will take advantage of the ignorant and push aside the incompetent. The struggle of education for a child is the struggle to overcome these two obstacles. Ignorance stifles us and keeps us from understanding why something is the way it is. It keeps us from appreciating the beauty of an idea, an expression of talent, or a piece of information that helps our lives. Incompetence is our inability to create or express or perform in some area, and it limits our achievement.

As in any battle, it takes courage to fight ignorance and incompetence because they are our natural states. We are born ignorant and incompetent. Life is a daily conquest of these two forces.

Ignorance and incompetence are countered by learning, and learning requires a teacher. The teacher can come in any form that communicates. It can be a book, a videotape, an audiotape, or a person. A teacher facilitates learning, directly or indirectly. Sometimes a teacher will teach the student the information or skill directly. At other times the teacher will show the student where to discover the information or acquire the skill.

In most classrooms, teachers use a combination of direct and indirect teaching. Your child's teacher may give a brief lecture about the subject and then have your child complete a worksheet that requires discovering answers in a book. To successfully learn in this situation, your child must demonstrate certain character qualities and attitudes, such as *obedience* to do the assignment, *curiosity* to seek out the answers, *diligence* to complete the work, *independence* to do the work on his own, and *neatness* to present a legible, finished product. You can help your child learn (and thus be a teacher) by encouraging the character and attitudes required for learning.

Encouragement and Homework

When your child comes to you for help on homework, it will most likely involve one or more of the areas listed below. You can diagnose the problem by examining each of these possibilities:

1. *He Does Not Understand the Directions.* If this is the case, read the directions together and ask the child what he thinks they mean. It may be that restating the directions in his own words will help. If it does, encourage him to read the directions more slowly next time and restate them out loud to himself.

   Encourage your child to be patient and analytical. You can do this by reminding him of other times when he demonstrated patience and the ability to analyze something. For example, you might say,

"David, when you read the directions it really helps to read them slowly and pick out each part of what the teacher wants you to do. I noticed the other day you did this when you were building your model airplane. I was proud to see your patience and attention to each part of the directions on that project, and I know you can do it on this homework assignment too."

2. *She Hasn't Mastered a Necessary Step in the Process.* All homework requires multiple steps. Review each step to find the one that may be causing the problem. In math, she may be skipping a step in calculating the answer. In social studies, she may not have developed the skill of connecting a historical event to causes or consequences and has trouble with questions involving why. In English class, she may not understand the skill of inferring meaning from the context or reading between the lines. Breaking down the homework into its steps and encouraging your child's ability to complete each step will give her courage to tackle the assignment.

You can encourage her to be orderly and methodical in each step of the assignment. Remind her of times when she has been orderly and methodical. As you watch her review each step you can look for any part that she struggles with or has not mastered. You can then either help her yourself or contact the teacher, explain the portion she struggles with, and ask the teacher to help her with it.

3. *He Lacks Confidence.* It may be that your child has the skill but lacks the confidence to use the skill because of fear of failure. You can infuse him with the courage to try by reminding him of his past achievements. Each success, no matter how small, will build greater confidence in your child. He may not realize the many successes he has had. That is why your encouragement is so powerful in equipping him with the emotional tools necessary to face

a new challenge on his homework with confidence.

Lawrence J. Greene, in his book *Kids Who Under-achieve*, writes:

> Challenges offer an opportunity for a child to learn how to use frustration constructively. By confronting challenges, he develops a sense of his own power and an appreciation for his own capabilities. He also learns about his strengths and weaknesses, and he discovers an important fact of life: he must work if he is to achieve. [1]

You can help your child appreciate his capabilities by reminding him of past accomplishments. Instill him with courage through encouragement.

4. *She Doesn't Like Working Alone.* It is sometimes the case that solitude in doing homework can be difficult for a child. It may be that your child simply wants the reassurance of your presence. Does your child want you near because she needs your constant assistance, or is it simply because she likes to be around others while she works independently? If it is the former, she should eventually work toward independence.

Here is an example of how to encourage your child:

Child: I'm stuck! This assignment is too hard.

Parent: I'm sure your teacher gave this to you with the confidence you could do it. Let's look at the directions at the top of the page. Read them to me.

Child: Fill in the map of the United States with the names of each state and use the chart on page 351 to label your map with the type of agriculture grown in each state.

Parent: What do you think the teacher wants you to do?

Child: Name each state and write in the agricul-
          ture grown in that state.

Parent: What do you think the teacher wants you
          to learn? [This question will enhance the
          learning.]

Child: I don't know. . . .

Parent: Think about it.

Child: The location of each state and what
          grows there?

Parent: That's right! You will also learn how to
          read a map and how to transfer informa-
          tion from a chart to a map. Now, locate
          the name of one state on the map in your
          book.

Child: Here's one—Florida.

Parent: Good. Notice the bold type used to spell
          Florida [teaching map-reading skills].
          The mapmaker used the same bold type
          for all the other states' names. Now,
          write the word "Florida" neatly on your
          map.

Child: So, what agriculture grows in Florida?

Parent: Where would you find that information?

Child: On page 351. Here it is! It shows or-
          anges, grapefruit, and peanuts.

Parent: So where on your map should you write
          the words oranges, grapefruit, and pea-
          nuts to indicate that they grow in Flor-
          ida?

Child: Inside the state.

Parent: Very good. I knew you could do it. You're
          good at searching out the answer like a
          detective [note the encouragement]. Do
          the next three states on your own, and
          I'll check your work.

(A few minutes later)

> Parent: Great job! You've found every one. And your teacher will really like it if you make sure that all the letters in your words are neat and straight. I'll bet you can do all of them on your own, and I'll check it when you're done.

Two Powerful Learning Enhancers

Resist the temptation to do the work for your child. Instead, encourage confidence in his own ability. Notice in the above example the two learning enhancers the parent used. First, she asked the child not only to explain what the teacher wanted him to do but also to explain what the teacher wanted him to learn. If a student understands what he is supposed to get out of the homework, he will be better prepared to learn it. Second, she enhanced her son's skill development by using what I call the power of "and." Let me explain these two enhancers.

What Are You Supposed to Learn?

This question reinforces in the student's mind that the purpose of doing homework is to learn something rather than just to get the assignment done. If a parent only shows concern that the homework is done, the message the child hears may be that speed and a grade are the only important factors in doing homework. When your child must think about and articulate to you what the teacher expects him to learn, he takes a more active role in learning. For instance, a vocabulary-building assignment is ultimately not about spelling words correctly and copying their definitions out of the dictionary. It is also about learning to use the dictionary and adding words to his functional vocabulary. It is possible that a student can accurately copy all the definitions for words on a vocabulary list without thinking about the words or their meanings at all. In this example, it is not enough that the student be a human copy machine; he must digest the words and understand the value in using them in his communication. Parents and teachers should not assume that students will automatically understand the connection between doing the assignment and learning something.

The Power of "And"

Notice in the parent-child conversation above that the parent's last comment added a skill-developing comment:

"And your teacher will really like it if you make sure that all the letters in your words are neat and straight." That is a technique for enhancing your child's performance by showing him how to do it better without diminishing what he has done.

The word *but* is used too often in correcting a student's work. Using it, we give a compliment and immediately follow it with a criticism. The parent might say, for instance, "Good job, but you need to be neater." The student might hear that as, "You really didn't do a good job." The word *and*, however, separates the two comments. "Good job, and you can make it even better by being neater." Using the word *and* shows a way to enhance a job that is already done well. I'm not suggesting that you strike the word *but* from your vocabulary. It is often necessary to use it to show contrast and comparison. Simply add the word *and* as a tool to more positively enhance your child's work.

Encouragement as a Character Builder

A vital part of your child's growth is the development of his character, and encouragement plays an essential role in the building of character. Your child's character—his inner personality—will shape the quality of his achievements and relationships throughout his life.

Encouraging good character in your child will help him resist peer pressure to make bad choices. As he sees himself develop as an honest or responsible or obedient person, he can better stand against the pull of negative peer pressure. He will not feel as strongly the need to find his identity from peers by doing wrong things, because you have helped him shape a better identity. *I'm more responsible than that,* he may think.

Parent, you are your child's mirror. He will see himself through the mirror of your feedback. When he sees himself, through your words, as responsible or self-controlled or respectful, he will be more prone to act that way.

In my book *Charting Your Family's Course*, I list numerous character qualities that your child can demonstrate.[2] Good character qualities are vital for success in school. On this foundation a child can more successfully build his skills and knowledge. Encourage your child to be:

Caring	Committed	Compassionate	Conscientious
Dependable	Energetic	Enthusiastic	Possessing Faith
Friendly	Goal-oriented	Good Listener	Encouraging
Hardworking	Honest	Imaginative	Intelligent
Knowledgable	Loving	Loyal	Organized
Neat	Persistent	Personable	Positive
Responsible	Humorous	Thoughtful	Wise
Obedient	Generous	Confident	Courageous
Fair	Understanding	Gentle	Optimistic

Dorothy Rich, in her book *MegaSkills*, shows how a child's demonstrated character can be exhibited as an adult:

Now—in school—Gordon enjoys tackling new projects and making new friends. Later—on the job—Mr. Smith does not shy away from hard jobs. He meets challenges head-on and has excellent interpersonal skills.

Now—in school—Becky gets her assignments in on time. Later—on the job—Ms. Stein meets her deadlines through effective resource management.

Now—in school—Alan has patience. He wants to keep at a task until it is done. Later—on the job—Mr. Johnson is a man who finishes what he starts. In our business, we call him the "closer." [3]

Those are habits of character: confidence, responsibility, and perseverance. You can encourage your child's character development by using the two-step technique that we have discussed: Recognize the behavior and reveal the character it demonstrates.

Encouragement and Self-Esteem

Many school districts have made self-esteem one of their top educational goals. But not all approaches to enhancing self-esteem actually achieve that goal. Unfortunately, there are thousands of schools using a variety of gimmicks in the hope of raising the level of student self-esteem. These are largely a waste of time and, ironically, take away time from activities that already increase healthy self-esteem.

Two Approaches to Self-Esteem

The misguided idea most frequently used in schools to justify self-esteem programs is based on the notion that self-esteem comes *before* achievement. The theory is that changes in self-concept/esteem cause changes in achievement.[4] When students feel good about themselves, the claim is that they will perform better. Based on this idea, teachers focus on activities that encourage self-discovery, and students turn inward to explore their feelings.

Examples of activities in student self-discovery abound. One school, for instance, has children make paper vests and paste on cut-out pictures of rock stars, animals, and other things to represent who they feel they are. A fifth-grade teacher in another school thinks she is enhancing student self-esteem by replacing classwork with games every Friday.[5] A parent told me that her son's school replaced the Pledge of Allegiance with a pledge to the Self. Each day students recite things like, "I am the one who shares, I am the one who cares; every day in every way I'm getting better, better, better; I, only I, can solve all the problems in my life." Still other schools have the children write journals and sit in circles to discuss their feelings.

That all sounds fun (or at least interesting), but there is little to no evidence that it raises self-esteem. The difficulty is that the self-esteem of a child entering school is largely already formed by the family, and schools have a limited impact on self-esteem.[6]

A better approach to enhancing self-esteem is based on the idea that self-esteem *comes from* achievement. Changes in achievement *cause* changes in self-concept and esteem. The teacher emphasizes developing student skills and knowledge. The teacher becomes the coach in guiding students to academic and behavioral success.

In the July 1991 issue of *The American School Board Journal*, professor Susan Black points out that research consistently shows that improved self-esteem is an outcome rather than a cause of success and achievement.[7] She analyzed more than one hundred publications on self-esteem from universities, education agencies, independent researchers, and school districts before concluding that many of the efforts initiated in our schools in the name of raising student self-esteem miss the mark entirely.

Additional support for the idea that places academic achievement as a major *cause* of enhanced self-concept is an extensive study done by two investigators who sought to prove that positive self-concept must come before academic achievement.[8] To their surprise, they had to conclude—after evaluating many programs and strategies that looked first to enhancing positive self-concept instead of academic achievement—that no causal relationship between self-concept changes and achievement could be found. They reported that the evidence favored the skills-development approach.

That is why it is so important that your child experience successes at school. He doesn't have to be a straight-A student, but he does need to see himself successfully making progress.

The Key to Self-Esteem at School

Education is not primarily about feeling good about oneself; it is about learning something. In the process of teaching skills and proficiency in academics, good teachers promote self-esteem. They do so by causing the student to find out something about himself: that he can learn and achieve.

Ironically, in forgetting the self and pursuing academic excellence, the student discovers himself as well. He finds that he has the ability to understand math, the creativity to express himself eloquently, or the skill to paint beautifully. His self-esteem increases *naturally*. But it increases in a way that will serve him throughout life because it is attached to feelings of worth about his character and his capabilities. *He has found success in something, and that discovery leads him to try achieving at the next level.* The teacher's role is to teach, not to encourage emotional introspection. The teacher's role is also to coach—to encourage, to inspire, and to maintain high expectations. Key ingredients in classrooms that promote healthy self-esteem include:

- Acceptance and respect for all students.
- High, yet reasonable, expectations.
- An emphasis on skills development.
- Love and care from the teacher.
- Students showing respect for one another.
- Grades are not equated with a student's worth.
- Recognition for making progress.

To insure that your child's self-esteem is developing in a healthy way, be sure that she is growing in her academic knowledge and skills. If the teacher does not challenge her enough, find out what she should be learning and what she should be able to do. Then, encourage her to "overachieve" in the classroom by going beyond the low expectations of the teacher. Maintain reasonable, yet high, expectations at home, and give her lots of encouraging comments. You might also explain to her that while this teacher may have an easy class the next teacher might not be so easy, and you don't want her to suffer once she is in the harder teacher's class.

If the teacher only uses grades to praise the students, send him a note pointing out a few positive indications of your child's growth that don't have to do with grades. For example:

Dear Mr. Smith,
    Ginger is making good progress in her study habits at home. She has shown greater self-discipline in sticking to her homework until it is completed, and she is more

conscientious about being neat. I'm encouraged by her development in these areas and wanted you to know that. I'm sure she'd appreciate an encouraging word in class on her progress.

That kind of note will indicate to the teacher that you are a supportive parent working with your child at home, and he will respect that. It will also encourage him to look beyond grades to skills and character. Since self-esteem at school is closely tied to making progress in academic skills, let's look at what you can do to help your child develop essential skills.

Encouragement as a Skill Developer

Just as you can help your child develop the character and emotional qualities necessary for success, so you can encourage skill development in your child as well. Academic competency comes through developing and using specific skills. No one is born with academic skills; they must be learned. You can help your child see himself as a skillful person by using the two-step process outlined above. However, instead of recognizing his behavior and revealing his character, recognize his behavior and reveal the skill he demonstrated.

When you help your child develop skills, you are providing him with an important ingredient for his self-esteem. When it comes to academics, healthy self-esteem is a result, not a cause, of achievement. As your child accomplishes success, his self-image increases. Skills are inseparably tied to achievement. Your child may have tremendous desire, but he must be taught the skills that can channel that desire into accomplishment. A few skills you can encourage are:

- Organized—able to create order from disorder
- Neat—able to write legibly, draw clearly, or keep his surroundings in order
- Comprehension—able to understand what he reads or is told
- Artistic—able to create and execute in the arts

- Mechanical—able to understand and manipulate machines and tools
- Athletic—able to perform physically in sports
- Problem-solver—able to find solutions and overcome hurdles
- Detailed—able to keep track of the details in a project
- Classification—able to put things in groups according to common factors
- Research—able to carefully study something using a variety of tools
- Summarization—able to condense something he reads to its essence
- Synthesis—able to bring together several ideas or facts to create a new whole
- Analytical—able to break down an issue or problem into its parts to be studied
- Concentration—able to maintain attention on a task

Try to develop an expanded list of skills that you can encourage in your child. Ask the teacher to help you by telling you what specific skills your child should use to successfully complete the homework. Place the list on your refrigerator or by your bedside. Go over your list again, and be ready to encourage specific skills.

An important part of being motivated is feeling successful. Your child may not appreciate how successful he is with certain skills because he sees only his current lack of success at achieving his larger goal of getting an A in the class. When you recognize how well he is demonstrating specific academic skills, you are helping him develop success orientation. He will begin to see the power he has to do better in his academics. Implement the techniques in this chapter, and you will see your child's self-confidence and achievement skyrocket. It will happen because you will have become an expert encourager!

Summary

Encouragement is a powerful tool for helping your child develop academically as well as morally. Unfortunately, even though it costs us nothing to give an encouraging word to our children, we sometimes find it difficult to give this long-lasting gift to them. The encouragement process involves two simple steps: recognizing your child's conduct and revealing his character and/or skills. Encouraging your child if he is struggling with his homework can be made easier by checking four things: He understands the directions, he understands each step in the homework process, he has confidence, and he can work independently. You can also help your child by encouraging him to see what he is supposed to get out of the homework. When correcting his work, try to focus on what he has done correctly, using the word *and* to add a comment about how he could improve his work. Remember, your child's self-esteem will be uplifted when he has achieved a goal or overcome an obstacle. Your encouragement—literally instilling courage—to succeed will have a lifelong impact on his success. The next chapter will show you how to boost your child's achievement by becoming excited about his studies yourself.

6
Boost Motivation

Parent Power Tool #4: Display Interest in Your Child's Subject

Your Goal

I read up on the subjects my child is studying. I look for real-world applications of his studies. I am genuinely enthusiastic about each subject and demonstrate this by things I say and do.

You may find that your child—especially your teenager—merely goes through the motions of learning at school. His focus is on the process: going to class, filling in worksheets, reading the books, and getting the grades. In this chapter you will learn how to get your child interested in the subject he is studying.

Education is like a bank; the more interest you show, the more your child will invest. When I refer to interest in the *subject,* I mean much more than merely making sure your child's homework is done. The homework is the process. Certainly, as I pointed out in the previous chapter, your child can learn much from the process of doing homework, but how do you get your child interested in the *subject* of math, English, or history?

Think for a moment about your own experience as a student. Most likely your interest in a particular subject fluctuated between boredom and interest based upon how interesting the teacher was. One history teacher droned on about details of history and assigned fill-in-the-blank worksheets every day. Another history teacher brought each historical character to life and had the students become detectives of the past. Her class brought surprise for the students almost every day, and the teaching method changed frequently. You could tell which teachers were truly interested in the subject and which ones were not. That interest, or lack of it, was broadcast to you as a student and affected the value you placed on the subject.

Your interest in the subjects your child is learning is key because you are more influential in your child's life than his teachers are. Your child looks to you for acceptance, love, and approval more than anyone else. He wants a close and loving relationship with you. Consequently, he will be interested in the things you enjoy because they become a shared experience—something that can deepen the parent-child bond. As he grows older, his interest can become more independent and self-generated.

We see this happen often in the area of sports. For example, Mr. Wilson and his high school-aged son, Todd, share a common interest in sports. As a toddler, Todd used to sit in his dad's lap and watch football and baseball games. His father played both football and baseball in high school and told Todd about his experiences in vivid and exciting detail. When Todd was very young his father signed him up for T-ball. They spent hours together tossing a baseball back and forth in the backyard. They went to many football and baseball games together. Dad explained each play and the strategies each team used. Todd began collecting baseball cards and hung sports posters on his bedroom walls. For Christmas and birthdays he always got something related to baseball or football. He started early in football too. Dad went to every Peewee game. He even coached on Todd's baseball and football teams. As Todd grew older, they read the sports page together and conversed on the recent sports news and statistics. Now in high school, Todd is on the varsity baseball team and is hoping for a scholarship to a college.

There is a good chance that your children will follow your footsteps in developing like interests, just as Todd did with his father. However, this pattern need not apply only to sports. The same principle of child-following-parent's interest can be applied to academic subjects as well.

The example of Todd illustrates four ways to generate your child's interest in an academic subject: (1) talk about the subject, (2) read about the subject, (3) make learning a priority in your home, and (4) apply the subject to the real world. Let's examine these four together.

Talk About the Subject

It seems obvious that if parents want to get their children interested in an academic subject they will talk about it. However, as I have counseled parents I have found that this is not being done enough. Talking about the subject goes well beyond the usual questions about whether or not your child completed his assignment. In fact, that is not talking about the subject at all. It is only focusing on the *process* of learning about the subject.

Our children generally become interested in the things we talk about. How much we talk about something sends a message of priorities to our children. If you want to know what someone values, thinks about, or dreams of, listen to what she talks about, how she talks about it, and how much she talks about it. Here is the acid test: How much and how enthusiastically do you talk about the subjects your child is learning?

Talking about the subject means conversing with your child about history, English, math, science, art, or whatever he is learning. To do that, you need to take some time to think about exactly what you can talk about. Here are some suggestions:

Talk About the Latest News Regarding the Subject.

In our sports example, Todd and his father were always reading the latest news concerning teams and players. It became a point of connection between them. The key is to create other points of connection. There is always some kind of news concerning every subject. Magazines like *Time* and *Newsweek* include stories on art, literature, science, and culture, as well as the usual political news. Your local newspaper will also have stories on these topics. Look for appropriate articles, and talk about them over dinner. You can even read them aloud to the family if they are short or read excerpts if they are longer.

Talk About the Superstars Involved in the Subject.

In our sports example, Todd learned to admire the heroes of sports. He admired the abilities of the superstar, hoping that someday he too could be like that.

Every academic field has its superstars. You can find adventure and, yes, money, in careers related to math, English, history, science, foreign languages, computers, or the arts. Who are the leading scientists in an area and what have they discovered? Do they travel the world in pursuit of their discoveries? Point out a writer who just signed a multimillion dollar contract with his publisher (you mean you can make money from succeeding in language arts class?). Talk about a businessman who was just named CEO of a large corporation and discuss the skills that got him the job (can schooling give your child those same skills?). This doesn't mean that money and fame need to be primary motivations for school. The point is to help your child see that success in school has real-world applications. Here are a few examples:

- Writer James Clavell received a $5,000,000 advance for his novel *Whirlwind*. (Relevant subjects: English and history)
- Computer-wiz Bill Gates revolutionized computing while building Microsoft, the largest software company in the world. (Relevant subjects: math, science, economics, computers)
- Clarence Thomas rose from humble origins to the Supreme Court. (Relevant subjects: history, English, and political science)

Relate Personal Experiences About the Subject.

Todd, in our example, listened intently while his dad told him exciting stories of his days on the playing field. Is it any wonder that the boy wanted to be like his dad as he got older by playing the same sports himself?

Unfortunately, when it comes to academic subjects, we sometimes tell our children of the frustrations and difficulties we had. Avoid telling your child how much you hated math or history. He may interpret that as a license to hate those subjects himself. Rather, tell him stories in which a subject helped you. Tell your children what subjects you enjoyed in school and why you enjoyed them. Were your vacations made more enjoyable by your knowledge of history? Were you able to spot an error on your bank account because of your math skills? Were you able to design an addition to your house partly by using geometry?

Ask Your Child Questions About the Subject.

In questioning your child about school subjects, you convey interest and bestow importance on the subject. It would be interesting to survey students about the importance of school in general and then specific subjects in particular. I speculate that most students would respond that school is important, but when pressed to say why a specific subject is important or relevant to their lives they would have more difficulty. This should be just the reverse, at least for older students. Instead of students only being able to say that a classroom activity is fun while being unable to explain why the subject matter is important, they should be able to explain why a subject is important and wonder whether or not the method of delivery at school is valuable ("I know I need to understand this math, but the teacher only uses worksheets and doesn't explain herself very well").

I imagine the difference is because parents routinely talk in a generally superficial and abstract manner about the importance of school and rarely talk about the significance of a specific subject. Asking your child about what he is learning will show your interest in the subject.

Go beyond merely asking, "What did you learn in school today?" to which your child may answer, "Nothing." Here are some sample questions you can ask your child about a subject or skill he is learning:

- What is the latest skill you learned in math [or other subject]? Can you demonstrate that skill to me?

- How well did you do on your science assignment? Which answers did you miss? What was the toughest question that you got right?
- If you were the teacher, how would you teach about the Industrial Revolution [or whatever he is studying]?
- Why do you think your English [or other] class is important?
- Will your teacher give you extra credit if we do something or go somewhere [involving the subject he is studying]? (Suggest a family field trip.)
- Do you think I would enjoy reading the book you are reading in your English class? Why or why not?

It is best to ask only a few questions in one setting. These discussions can take from two to five minutes. Your child may shy away from having discussions about school if you force the issue and engage in long talks. Choose a time to talk that is natural when your child is not distracted by other thoughts or activities. Also, realize that he may not be in the mood to talk when you are. Finally, make clear that you are asking these questions because you are interested in the subject and in your child's progress. If he thinks you are evaluating him or trying to catch him doing poorly, he may avoid such conversations altogether.

Read About the Subject

As I mentioned before, read magazine and newspaper articles on events and people surrounding the subjects your child is learning. This will help you talk about the real-world applications of the subject.

Another way to show interest in what your child is learning is to get an extra copy of his textbook and read it. Your child's teacher will be pleasantly surprised if you ask to borrow a copy of the textbook so you can read along. If your child is in middle school or high school, you might get textbooks from each class. Don't try to read the books from cover to cover. Instead, simply keep up with the reading your child is doing or the chapter covering the lessons in class. It will only take a short amount of time each night. Make a habit of reading or skimming a few pages before going to bed.

You can also read the novels or stories he reads for class. Jolene, a mother of a middle-school boy, told me that her son appreciated it when she read the books he read in English class. "Sometimes after he reads a good book, or even while he's reading it, he'll recommend it to me. Sometimes I'll say, 'That looks interesting, I'd like to read it when you're done.' I can sense that he feels proud that he introduced me to something we can enjoy together."

Four things will happen because of this:

1. You will visibly demonstrate the importance of learning the subject by showing interest in it. Children imitate their parents. If you show interest in a subject, your child's interest may also increase.
2. You will be able to better converse about the subject with your child. School is to a child what a job is to an adult. By conversing about the subjects of his work, you show an interest in your child's world. You can do this over dinner, after school, before bed, or whenever the moment is right. Here are a couple of suggestions for starting a conversation about an academic subject:

   "I really enjoyed the textbook's section on _____

   because I never realized _____."
   "I learned something new today . . ." [tell what you learned].

3. You will be better equipped to help him with homework. As an adult, you already have a greater ability to solve problems. You have had many years of practice with reading and following directions and analyzing the source of problems. By reading about

the subject you will be able to more precisely help your child. You will better understand the context of the homework and be able to guide your child accordingly.

4. You will learn something yourself. Discovering new things is fun. You will sharpen your own knowledge, which can be useful in *your* life. You will become more interesting in your conversations with your friends and colleagues. Most adults haven't picked up a history book or a literary work since their days in school. You will have a knowledge of history, literature, science, art, and culture at your fingertips. You will also be able to fill in the gaps of your own education. Did the multiplication of fractions confuse you when you were in school? Now you have an opportunity to overcome that old hurdle. Have you always wondered exactly where to use commas in your own writing at work or in letters? Reading your child's grammar book will enable you to write with more confidence.

If your child's teacher is not using a textbook for a particular unit or you cannot get a copy of a textbook, you can find a good book on the subject at the public library. Going to the library to get subject-related books is another way to show interest in your child's academic subjects. Even though you may not have time to read an entire book on a given subject, you can still help your child. For instance, your child may be learning about pioneers crossing the Oregon Trail. There are many books on this subject in the library. Here are a few tips on how to select a book and quickly read about a topic such as the Oregon Trail:

- Get a book on the general history of the West in the 1800s, and use the index to zero in on the sections about the Oregon Trail.

- Get a book on pioneers in general, and read the chapter that deals with those pioneers who crossed the Oregon Trail.
- Get a book that specifically covers the Oregon Trail, and read a few specific stories of those who traveled on the trail. These may be different stories from those your child reads, and you can make the subject more interesting by retelling these stories at the dinner table.

Make Learning a Priority in Your Home

You can help your child generate interest in an academic subject by the priorities you set in your home. When we consciously make priorities, we place those things that are of most importance to us at the top of the list. Learning should be one of those priorities. There are several ways you can demonstrate to your child that learning an academic subject is a priority in your family.

Establish a Quiet Place for Homework

If learning is important, it should be respected with a special place. Set up an office for your child—his own place for studying. Be sure that it is well lit and has a desk large enough to spread out his work. He will need some bookshelves. You may want to consider a small filing cabinet or box for storing completed and graded homework assignments. Removing old assignments from his notebook and storing them will avoid the problem of having too many papers stuffed in his notebook and creating a mess.

Be sure that your child's office is in a quiet place. Television and loud radio will be distracting. However, music playing softly may help your child concentrate. Your child may not study under the same conditions that you prefer. Some children need absolute silence. Others find silence unnerving. The key is to evaluate what works best for your child and then provide it for him.

Have a Disciplined Homework Routine

This will vary with each child. Some students work on homework best immediately after school. Others need a break from school and can work best before or just after dinner. Late-night homework cramming is not good. Not only is it the worst time for mental freshness, but it also establishes in the student's mind that schoolwork is of little importance and can be done at the last minute.

For a young child it might be a good idea to set up a daily schedule of activities. Have the schedule start when your child comes home from school and end with bedtime. Block time slots into half-hour segments. It is important that you establish the schedule with your child's input. For the schedule to be most effective, he must take ownership of the allotted times.

Here is an idea that may work well with your child or teenager. Establish a regular block of time—one or two hours—for homework every day. Have your child study during that time *whether he has any new homework or not.* This creates the habit of study and the expectation that he will be studying something every day at home. If he doesn't have new homework to study during this time, he can review material for an upcoming test, read ahead of the class, do an extra-credit assignment, or complete a homework-related project you have outlined at home. We want students to get in the habit of studying, yet we reward them with extra play time if they have no homework. Having consistent study time each day will mean that when your child does not have homework he will have an opportunity to get a better grade in class because he can do extra-credit work or study for an upcoming test.

Review Your Child's Homework

Another way to demonstrate that learning is a priority in your home is to review your child's homework regularly. You show your interest in his learning by getting involved in it. When your child sees you reviewing his work, he senses a strong message from you: *Your achievement is important to me.* There are three basic things to look for in reviewing his work: It is done completely, it is done neatly, and it is done on time.

It Is Done Completely. Check to see that the work conforms to at least the minimum requirements set forth by the teacher. Did your child follow all the instructions properly? For instance, the teacher's instruction may read, "Write a one-page creative story and incorporate the ten new vocabulary words from list number fifteen. Underline each of the vocabulary words in your story." Checking your child's work in this example requires several elements: Is the story at least one page in length? Does it use all ten vocabulary words? Is each word underlined? Are the vocabulary words used appropriately or merely stuck in the story awkwardly? Doing the homework completely means following all the instructions.

Sometimes a student will misinterpret the teacher's instructions. For instance, the teacher may want your child to exhibit the critical thinking skills of independent analysis. The question may read, "Why did the man in the story tell Cynthia that his dog was too old to obey his commands?" Your child may assume the teacher wants a literal answer, such as, "Because the dog didn't obey his master." However, the context of the story may warrant a more complete answer that shows your child's creative analysis, such as, "The man meant that for too many years the dog was used to disobeying his master without any consequences, so now the man didn't even expect him to be obedient." Doing the homework completely means interpreting the homework questions correctly.

Another problem for students that demotivates them occurs when the teacher doesn't give them clear direction to complete an assignment. Terri is a mom who finds that her daughter gets frustrated and loses enthusiasm for the project when this happens.

She told me, "Sometimes the teacher isn't clear about how to do the assignment. For instance, the other day my daughter had to do a report on Italy. The teacher gave her an outline on what to have in the report, but she didn't explain how to track down the information. My daughter quit in frustration. I took her to the public library and explained how to pull out the relevant facts for the report from a number of sources. Once she saw how she could do it she was motivated to finish her work."

Another common problem I see in students' work is writing incomplete sentences. When reviewing your child's homework, you may notice he starts his answer in midsentence. The usual word that signals this is "because." Your child's answer may read, "Because the cat ran up the tree to get away from the dog." A more complete answer might read, "The cat was stuck in the tree because it ran up the tree to get away from the dog." Sometimes doing homework completely means writing in complete sentences.

It Is Done Neatly. Any secondary teacher can tell you the sad state of penmanship among many students. Often boys write with a combination of printing and cursive strokes; their letters have a halting, scratchy, and juvenile appearance. Many girls write with a looping cursive stroke that projects a childish, even silly image. Penmanship projects to the reader something more about the writer than just what he wrote on the page. Good penmanship conveys the image of crisp thinking and thoughtful expression of an idea. Poor penmanship not only makes it difficult for the teacher to read what the student has written, it may convey to the teacher that your child isn't thinking clearly or is not serious about the assignment.

When looking for neatness keep in mind the level of your child's ability. Young children will have more difficulty with the fine motor skills needed for neat handwriting. As they get into upper elementary grades, however, you should be able to insist on clear handwriting.

Cursive is a form of writing in which the letters connect in a flowing manner. Some of the most common problems in student penmanship come from three areas: (1) use of printing almost exclusively, (2) combining printing and cursive in the same sentence or word, (3) poor execution of cursive. All three of these problems stem from lack of practice in cursive writing.

If your child exhibits problems with poor penmanship, set aside time to have him practice writing. Each stroke is simply a matter of hand-eye coordination that takes practice to do correctly. Here are steps you can take to help your child improve his penmanship.

1. Give him a model of good penmanship. At the top of a piece of ruled paper, neatly write each letter of the alphabet, but group them according to the initial stroke used to create the letter. Letters that use an initial downward overcurve moving the pen from right to left are: *a, c, d, o, g,* and *q*. Letters that use an initial upward undercurve moving the pen from left to right are: *b, e, f, h, i, j, k, l, p, r, s, t, u,* and *w*. Finally, there are letters that use an initial upward overcurve moving the pen from left to right: *m, n, v, x, y,* and *z*. Make each letter one-half inch high so the child can easily see the strokes involved.[1]

2. Give him several sheets of ruled paper, and have him practice each group of stroke-related letters. He should begin by writing the letters one-half inch high. Let him practice each group a dozen times or more. Be sure his letters do not become too loopy and make, for instance, an *i* look like an *e* with a dot above it. He should also avoid the opposite problem of having letters that are too closed and, for instance, make an *e* look like an *i*.

3. Give him ample opportunity to practice his newly learned skill in real-world applications beyond the drills. You might suggest he write a short letter to a relative and practice his skill. Have him use proper penmanship on the next homework assignment. Check his work regularly to critique his penmanship as well as the answers to his homework. Elegant penmanship helps your child communicate clearer and project an image of being a student who is conscientious about his work. His teacher will appreciate and reward him for it.

It Is Done on Time. Getting homework done on time requires time management habits that will help your child in school and for the rest of his life. Your child must do three things to make sure his homework is turned in on time: (1) he must clearly understand the assignment and its due date; (2) he must plan enough time to work on the assignment at a comfortable pace; and (3) he must remember to take his finished homework to school the day it is due.

If your child is in secondary school, he should have a place to record all his assignments as they are given. This can be a separate notepad or a designated page in his notebook. He needs to record the assignment requirements, the date the assignment was given, and the date it is due. If he has a problem remembering his homework assignments, ask the teacher to initial his homework notepad each day. I have seen many schools use this practice effectively for forgetful students. If he has no homework one day, he should write "no homework" for his records and have the teacher sign it. This simple procedure will enable you to hold him accountable for his homework. If he comes home and tells you he has no schoolwork to do, he must prove it by showing the signature(s) of his teacher(s) attesting to his assertion.

Many students fail to plan enough time to complete their homework with quality. Thoughtful planning is an important life skill that your child needs to learn. Homework assignments afford good opportunities to learn this skill. Too often students who have a week to work on an assignment wait to do it the night before it is due. If your child has this problem, he may need your help in dividing the work into shorter steps and being disciplined to complete each one.

For instance, if he has one week to complete an assignment, sit down with him and ask him to show you where he can divide the work into six equal parts (assuming he takes one day off over the weekend). On a separate paper list the descriptions of the actions that must be taken to complete the homework. As he completes each step, you can place a check next to its description on the list. If he has trouble being disciplined enough to stick with the schedule, you may want to devise a system of modest rewards for him, such as television privileges or time with friends. The key is to help him create a habit of dividing larger tasks into smaller action steps and being disciplined enough to complete each step.

Once he has completed his homework, he must remember to take it to school and turn it in on time. This can be accomplished by having him review his homework notepad each morning before leaving for school. If he has faithfully kept a record of his assignments and their due dates, he should have no problem with this.

Making learning a priority in your home is important for demonstrating your interest in your child's learning. The cliché is true, your actions *will* speak louder than your words. Providing a quiet and adequately equipped place for him to do his schoolwork, helping him establish a homework routine, and reviewing his work are all strong indicators of the high priority you set on learning.

Apply the Subject to the Real World

The more meaningful and relevant the subject is to your child, the faster and better she will learn it. Finding meaning in a subject helps create interest, and interest helps facilitate learning. Often teachers require students to learn something without explaining why the subject is important or relevant. Why read this story? Why learn this math formula? Why understand about this foreign country? I'm sure you have heard those questions from your children. When you answer them effectively you can generate in your child new interest for learning.

Listed below are a few ideas for promoting meaningfulness in academic subject matters. These ideas are by no means exhaustive, but they may inspire you regarding the subjects' relevance to your child's learning.

English

Why does your child need to learn about nouns, verbs, and prepositional phrases? Why is grammar important? Success in English class is important because it is about communication. One of the things that sets us apart from animals is our ability to articulate our thoughts and emotions in a precise manner. An animal may be able to communicate that he is angry, but he cannot write a poem to express that anger. God gave us the gift of language as a means to express our thoughts and feelings. To be understood is an important part of our sense of self.

Effective use of language means that we are not limited by our own experience. We do not need to discover every truth and error on our own. We can learn from others' successes and mistakes because they can relate them to us through language, spoken or written. We can proceed from where they left off.

Vocabulary building is important because you cannot think beyond your vocabulary. The voice in your head that expresses your thoughts draws on your own vocabulary. Having a broader vocabulary means you have more tools to use in forming thoughts and understanding other people's thoughts. This, of course, will help greatly in all areas of education.

The English language has conventions of spelling, grammar, and syntax. English class is designed to help your child learn it and confidently use it. Language is like money; it is a medium of exchange. To be poor in language is to be destitute in your ability to interact with your culture. Language arts class helps your child think more clearly, speak and write more effectively, and listen and read with greater understanding.

As your child matures in the use of language, he or she can move from simply comprehending what is written on the page to understanding what can be drawn from the author's message. We sometimes call that *reading between the lines*. This advanced use of language could be classified as higher-order thinking. It involves understanding such things as analogies, connotations, inferences, and symbolism. When your child uses those skills, she is asking deeper questions of and receiving deeper answers from the author or speaker.

Confident use of language has practical application in activities such as writing letters, songs, reports or memos on the job, speeches, or books. A masterful command of language can be used in a career in advertising, public relations, or journalism. You can introduce your child to people who rely on English for a career:

- Visit the offices of your local newspaper and watch how it is created.
- Visit an advertising agency and see how ad copy is written.
- Talk about your favorite authors.
- Visit a local publishing company and see how books are produced.
- Visit your pastor and ask him to show your child how he prepares a sermon.

History

Your child may ask why he must learn about "all those dead guys." Why is a study of the past important? Few students understand that studying history teaches the skill of combining facts with meaning. The student must discipline his mind to search for historical facts. Questions arise in the process, such as what are facts and what are opinons, what are relevant facts and what are not, and how wide must the field of investigation be spread in order to understand the context of the historical event?

Your child's history class teaches skills of investigation, objectivity and detachment, logic, sequential thinking, and the ability to move his perspective between the big picture and the single event. To write a report for history class, your child must select a topic and choose from what angle he will approach the topic. He must gather his sources and make judgments about what is important to include and what is not. He must exercise logic in writing a report that makes sense. These are invaluable skills.

In addition, every subject in school has a history. Math, science, and language arts all have a past. In fact, you could say that most of your child's learning is, in one sense, historical. When he learns a mathematical equation, for instance, he is not creating it, but he is learning a procedure that was developed in the past.

History is not just about facts; it is about gaining meaning from the facts. Questions arise concerning historical meaning, such as, What factors will shed new meaning on the event? Is the student imposing meaning on the event or drawing meaning from the event? And what bias does the student bring to the subject?

You can see an example of how history gives us a sense of context in the record-breaking goal of hockey superstar Wayne Gretzsky. Suppose you knew nothing of hockey but on a whim decided to attend a game. At the game you see Gretzsky score a goal. The crowd breaks out in wild cheers and the game stops. The players—even those from the opposing team—are congratulating Gretzsky. Without a sense of context you wouldn't know what to make of the commotion. Once you learned that he had broken Gordie Howe's career record of 801 goals you could appreciate the historic event with fresh excitement. History provides meaning.

A knowledge of history and the skills necessary for investigating it not only teach your child to appreciate his world, but they teach your child to think critically about who he is, where he fits in this world, and how he will live his life.

You can introduce your child to real-world applications of history in the following ways:

- Get a book that explains the historical origins of phrases such as "a chip off the old block" or "toe the line."
- Trace your family tree.
- Discuss the historical context for a recent news event.
- Read a book on the history of a place where you will take a family trip. Kelly, a mother of an eighth-grader, found that vacations were good times to make history come alive. One year they drove from Wisconsin to Yellowstone National Park and throughout Arizona. "Jordon was fascinated with Indian history and read *Dances with Wolves* while we traveled. Indian history came alive for him during our trip."
- Visit a businessman who has had to investigate the recent history of his industry in order to write a business plan or make business decisions.

Geography

The course of human development has followed the course of rivers, valleys, and seashores. Great cities grew along the edges of oceans and seas. Trade routes followed plains, passable mountains, and rivers. Farming developed on land that made it possible. Geography is the study of the way the environment promotes and inhibits the process of life on earth. It encompasses the sciences of meteorology, climatology, hydrology, oceanography, geology, and through plant geography, it can include botany.

Geography is related to such everyday activities as map reading, airplane flights, weather reports, agricultural produce in grocery stores, recreational fishing, hiking, and other outdoor recreation. You can help your child see the value of geography by:

- Making a game of asking where certain foods come from in the grocery store.
- Letting your child be the navigator with the map while traveling in the car.
- Discussing how weather conditions affect your family activities.
- Visiting local aquariums, farms, the Coast Guard, or ranger stations and talking to people there about local geography.

Mathematics

The subject of math can be a frustrating mystery for many students. It is a language in its own abstract world. In many ways math seems unrelated to everyday life. Its grammar is based on logic. Its vocabulary is made of symbols such as numerals for numbers, letters for unknown numbers, and equations for showing the relationship between numbers. Once beyond simple arithmetic your child may ask, "When will I ever use this?"

Theoni Pappas is the author of *The Joy of Mathematics* and *More Joy of Mathematics*. These two books show hundreds of ways that math is applied to life. For instance, she points out the role of math in tracking earthquakes by the waves they produce. Earthquakes produce three different types of waves (P, S, and L waves) which travel at different speeds and have different characteristics. Seismologists can pinpoint the epicenter of an earthquake by charting when the different waves reach various seismographs located throughout an area.

To make math more practical for your child, you can point out that when you balance your checkbook you are applying arithmetic. If you build a wall around your backyard, you are using techniques of geometric measurement. Every manmade object you have in your house represents principles of math in its design or function. Insurance companies use calculus—a system for analyzing change and motion—to determine the cost of a policy for people at different ages. Police investigators use algebra when looking at skid marks on the road to determine how fast a car was moving just before an accident.

Math-related activities that create relevance could include such things as:

- Visiting an architect, an engineer, an actuary, a medical researcher, a carpenter, a banker, an accountant, a pilot, a marketing executive, or anyone who deals with numbers, designs, tabulations, or calculations.
- Pointing out the geometry used in constructing a building: angles, circles, squares, right triangles, and arcs.
- When appropriate, showing your child how you handle the family finances.

Science

Probably the most obvious and easiest subject to apply to the world around you is science. We live in a scientific age. Our society is driven by the practical application of scientific technology. We see science in the launching of a rocket and in the running of our car's engine. We hear of scientific discoveries in the news on a regular basis. Because science involves discovery in mostly concrete ways, it is ready-made to capture your child's curiosity. Your child may not have difficulty understanding why studying science is important—its everyday application through technology may provide a strong enough stimulus to study this subject.

You can see science exhibited in the way electricity comes from a plug in the wall to your toaster and generates heat which browns your child's toast without actually touching it. You can see it in how electricity can come from the same plug and be directed to a lamp, which gives light to the room. Science is demonstrated when magnets interact with metal, clouds form in the sky, a plant grows, or detergents clean clothes.

Science is also one way of seeing the world around us. It teaches your child such skills as logic, observation, objectivity, experimentation, and calculation. You can find practical applications of why science is important in many areas. Here are a few suggestions:

- Visit a hospital or medical laboratory.
- Visit a factory to see how technology is used.
- Visit an electrical power plant.
- Go to a museum or aquarium.
- Take a tour of a farm and see how technology is used.
- Get a book on science experiments you can perform at home and have fun together creating an experiment.
- Visit a nursery and examine the variety of flowers.

Attitudes as Motivators

I know that in the real world of parenting it is sometimes the case that you cannot arouse in your child a genuine interest for a particular subject. In that instance, a lesson on attitude may help. Attitudes for success in school also relate to success in the world outside the classroom, and you can talk about this with your children. Sarah, a mother of six children told me, "We try to help our kids see that having a good attitude and motivation in school is similar to what a job requires. My husband hires a lot of people in his work, and he uses his experience to show the children how important attitude is in getting and keeping a job. Many times you have to do things in life that you don't like to do, but you do them anyway. And you have to do them well. The real world requires being internally motivated with a cheerful attitude."

Summary

One of the best ways to motivate your child's interest in an academic subject is to show interest in it yourself. Four key ways to show interest are to (1) talk about the subject, (2) read about the subject, (3) make learning a priority in your home, and (4) look for ways that the subject applies to the real world.

You can talk about the subject by asking questions of your child and discussing your own experiences or interests in the subject. You make learning a priority in your home by helping your child set a disciplined homework routine and by having high yet reasonable performance expectations. You can apply the subject to the real world by looking for ways that the academic subject is used in various professions and activities. *Ask the teacher to help you think of practical ways the subject applies to life.*

Reading a variety of materials will also help your child see how a subject applies to life. In the next chapter you will learn how to make reading a priority in your home.

Maximize Reading

Power Tool #5: Maximize Reading at Home

Your Goal
Everyone in the family reads something nearly every day. We talk about what we are reading, and I read to my child regularly and frequently. We demonstrate that reading is important by our actions.

Have you ever had the frustrating experience of helping your child answer questions about a book he is reading, and he can't quite seem to get the right answer? You give him a little hint of where to look for the answer in the passage, but he doesn't get it. You give him a bigger hint. He still doesn't get it. Finally, you explain what the answer should be. "Oh," he says, finally recognizing the connection between the question and the text. The problem here is a lack of mature reading skills.

Your child needs to read well to be successful in school. It may be that, as a family, you do not emphasize reading very much. Reading may seem so natural in everything you do that once your child masters the basic skill of decoding words, you may assume that it does not need to be emphasized anymore. WARNING: *If your view is that reading is only a process of decoding words, your view is inaccurate.* Don't put reading in the same category as learning to use a knife and fork—once mastered, it need not be improved upon. In this chapter, I will explain why mature reading is important to mature learning and how you can maximize your child's reading ability.

Reading starts with decoding a string of letters on a page to arrive at the meanings of words and sentences. Mature reading, however, involves much more. It develops important intellectual skills in your child.

As a student becomes more proficient in reading, he develops abilities for analyzing the logic of information—fact or opinion, logical or illogical, rational or emotional. Mature reading involves the ability to analyze the subtle aesthetics of information—beautiful or gaudy, clever or clownish, romantic or mushy. Reading requires the intellectual skills of conceptualizing abstract ideas versus concrete images. For instance, what I have written in this chapter so far are abstract ideas about reading. I have not used any pictures to illustrate a student using his thinking skills to read. Pictures, diagrams, and vividly drawn illustrations can help us all in understanding abstract ideas, but reading does not require these devices. When a child first learns to count, he may need physical objects to illustrate the abstract number. He uses his fingers to see that one plus one equals two. As he develops the ability to count, he no longer needs to count on his fingers. Because of the common denominator of the ability for abstract thinking, it is no wonder that students who have a high proficiency in reading also often do well in mathematics.

The written word communicates meaning. Each sentence contains a fact, a question, an assertion, or an explanation, or else it is meaningless. When your child reads a sentence, he must, in a split second, discern what it is, what it means, and how it fits into the context of the passage. He must retain that information in his short-term memory and know where to apply it in other parts of the text. He must make judgments about the reading: Is it true? Is it relevant? Is it valuable?

Mature readers learn to read between the lines. They can make inferences—a conclusion about the unknown based on what is known. They can recognize the tone of the writer and distinguish, for instance, between sincerity and sarcasm. They can put the message in their own words without changing its meaning. They can bring two thoughts together—synthesis—which may not be explicitly connected in the written passage.

To help your child improve his reading, you have to know about the various levels of reading ability. Once you know where you want your child to go, the path to get there becomes clearer.

How Skilled Is Your Child's Reading?

I have found that many parents have only a vague idea of their children's reading ability. In this section we will look in detail at what a student should be able to do at different reading levels. As you read each description, think about what your child is reading successfully and how well your child answers questions about what she has read.

The U.S. Department of Education's Office of Educational Research and Improvement has identified five categories for evaluating student reading levels: rudimentary, basic, intermediate, adept, and advanced.[1]

Rudimentary

Readers who have acquired rudimentary reading skills can follow brief written directions. They can also select words, phrases, or sentences to describe a simple picture. They can understand uncomplicated passages and correctly answer straightforward questions about what they read. For example, if a book has a picture of a dog in a doghouse, a child reading at a rudimentary level can correctly select the answer, "The dog is lying inside the doghouse" from a list of options that might include "on top of the doghouse" and "next to the doghouse."

You may be wondering how your child ranks in relation to other students around the nation. The U.S. Department of Education reports that 93 percent of nine year olds, 99.8 percent of thirteen year olds, and 100 percent of seventeen year olds surveyed read at this level.

Basic

Readers who have learned basic comprehension skills can locate and identify facts from simple informational paragraphs, stories, and news articles. In addition, they can combine ideas and make inferences based on short, uncomplicated passages. They can also summarize main ideas of simple passages. A student reading at this level could, for example, read a short passage about how to avoid poison ivy which includes a description of the plant and be able to identify the correct description of poison ivy from a list of other plant descriptions. However, readers at this level have difficulty answering questions about specific facts when they are in a passage using complex sentences.

The education department indicates that 62.5 percent of nine year olds, 95.1 percent of thirteen year olds, and 98.9 percent of seventeen year olds surveyed perform at this level.

Intermediate

Readers with intermediate skills can search for, locate, and organize information in passages containing four or five paragraphs and can recognize paraphrases of what they have read. They can also interpret, make inferences and reach generalizations about main ideas and an author's purpose from passages dealing with literature, science, and social studies.

For instance, let's suppose an intermediate reader reads about the history of basketball. Among many facts in the story, he reads that basketball was invented in 1891 as an alternative to football. The reader would be able to answer correctly that basketball was invented after football even though the passage does not specifically say that.

Seventeen percent of nine year olds, 58 percent of thirteen year olds, and 86.2 percent of seventeen year olds function at that level.

Adept

Readers with adept reading comprehension skills can understand stories with longer and more complex sentences. They can also analyze and integrate less familiar material and provide reactions to and explanations of the text as a whole. If your child is performing at this level, he has the ability to find, understand, summarize, and explain relatively complicated information.

For instance, suppose an adept reader reads a two-page history of the suffrage movement in America. In the passage, there is a lengthy quote from a woman responding to a man's claim that if women had the right to vote they would lose their charm. In the quote she argues that if women could work all day in factories without losing their charm, they could certainly vote without losing their charm. An adept reader would be able to summarize the woman's quote and select the correct generalization of her message from a list of possible answers.

Only 1.2 percent of nine year olds and 10.6 percent of thirteen year olds perform at this level, whereas 41.8 percent of seventeen year olds surveyed are adept readers.

Advanced

Readers who use advanced reading skills can extend and rephrase the ideas presented in texts that use long and complex sentences. They are also able to understand the links between ideas even when those links are not explicitly stated and to make appropriate generalizations even when the texts lack clear introductions or explanations. This is the level of reading necessary for many books your child will read in college. For instance, a reader at this level would be able to rephrase and comment on the meaning of a complex sentence such as, "Members of the Court, applying general constitutional provisions, understandably differ on occasion as to their meaning and application."

If your teenager is performing at this level, she is demonstrating the ability to learn from specialized or technical reading materials. She can also answer open-ended questions and express her own ideas based on the passage.

Two-tenths of 1 percent of thirteen year olds and a meager 4.8 percent of seventeen year olds performed at this level.

An Additional Perspective on Comprehension

In order to help your child it is essential that you understand what various reading levels look like, which is why I outlined each level of reading as categorized by the U.S. Department of Education. But I also want you to see comprehension skills from the perspective of a classroom teacher and reading specialist. This will help you gain further insight into how your child should be developing. Terry Salinger offers a helpful perspective on judging reading comprehension. In her book *Language Arts and Literacy for Young Children,* she outlines four levels.[2] Your child may demonstrate each one of these skills but with varying sophistication depending on his age.

1. Literal Comprehension

This is the most basic level. It involves recognizing and recalling specific facts or details of what is read. Mastery of this literal comprehension means your child reads carefully and remembers what he reads. He is operating at the literal level when the teacher assigns questions whose answers are directly stated in the text. Those are sometimes called "right there" questions because the answers are right there in the text.

Learning Tip: If your child is in secondary school and is bringing home worksheets that require only literal comprehension, his abilities are not being developed.

2. Inferential Comprehension

This skill involves understanding what the author implied in the writing. It moves beyond the surface meaning of the text. Your child uses inferential comprehension when he thinks about hidden meanings or relationships within (or outside) the text. As he reads, he asks, "Does the text imply something more than what is written?" The teacher is challenging him to make inferences when she gives him assignments that require him to draw conclusions that are not directly stated in the text.

Learning Tip: Unless your child is a beginning reader, be sure he is being challenged to make inferences. If he is not, you can use discussions at home to help him do that.

3. Evaluative Comprehension

This skill requires making judgments about the text. Your child should also be able to evaluate a text for accuracy, worth, completeness, or usefulness. Your child is using evaluative comprehension skills when she expresses an opinion about what she has read.

Learning Tip: Questions that ask "What do you think?" require your child to use the comprehension skill of evaluation. You can help your child develop this skill by asking his opinion on something he read.

4. Appreciative Comprehension

This skill involves the previous three levels of comprehension and adds an emotional interaction with the text. Your child is displaying appreciative comprehension when he gets angry at a character in the story or is delighted by something the character does. He is also demonstrating appreciative comprehension when he can express awareness of the author's use of various writing techniques in developing plot, characters, and setting in the story. He may say, "I like how the author brought the two boys back together again after they got separated." That shows an appreciation that is detached from the story and directed toward the author himself.

Learning Tip: You can help your child develop this skill by discussing a story with him and asking him what he liked about the way it was written.

As you can see, reading is more than recognizing words on a page. If you can recognize words without comprehending the real meaning of a sentence or paragraph, word recognition isn't the problem, higher-order thinking is. To be a mature reader also requires an awareness of information outside the text. It requires a background in our culture—a sense of context.

Context and Culture

You may find that your child recognizes the individual words in a text but has trouble with the meaning of the sentence or paragraph because she lacks a *context* for understanding. For instance, you might read: "What was missing in their relationship was the application of the Golden Rule."

You understand perfectly well what each word means. You know the definitions of *missing, relationship, application, golden*, and *rule*. But without understanding the Golden Rule, you will have no idea what was missing from their relationship.

In another instance, your teenager may read an article satirizing the Congress of the United States. The author uses subtle wit and exaggeration to make her point. In order to understand the meaning, your child will need to know, at least somewhat, the real state of affairs in Congress to understand the satire and not mistake the piece for a news report.

This skill requires a sense of context. In order to comprehend what he is reading, your child must have a storehouse of background knowledge. He may be able to sound out the words in a passage but may have no idea of its meaning because he lacks an awareness of the culture behind it.

To function well in our society, we need to have a high level of cultural literacy. Many young people are not fluent enough in our cultural foundations to function at advanced levels. This may be one of the strongest arguments for learning what appears, at first, to be useless information. Shakespeare may not have any direct relevance to your child's everyday life. Certainly she can get along sufficiently without having any knowledge of the playwright. But Shakespeare is a part of our cultural fabric, and writers quote lines from his plays often. It is one more thread in our cultural clothing. To extend the metaphor, too many students are in an appalling state of cultural undress.

Here are some tips you can use to cultivate your child's cultural literacy:

- Be sure your child reads a variety of material appropriate for his age such as the Bible, magazines, classic stories, and the newspaper.
- Be sure your child is regularly learning something about history. You can encourage this through conversing at dinner, reading an interesting story, visiting a museum, going to a historical site, or watching a television show or video about a historical event.
- Expose your child to a variety of activities in our culture such as musicals, operas, plays, folk festivals, ethnic fairs, home shows, gardening conventions, and

sports events. The richer his experiences, the more he can bring to his reading.

How to Maximize Reading Skills

You can do four specific things at home to maximize your child's ability at home. They are: reading aloud, encouraging your child to demonstrate mature reading skills, having a balanced reading diet, and using the library effectively.

Reading Aloud

Reading aloud to your young children is a good way to introduce them to the sounds and meanings of words. It also helps them see that books are written to convey stories and messages—that reading is for gaining meaning and under-standing. Reading aloud to your children makes a priority of reading. The emotional warmth and bonding that goes along with the read-aloud experience is important.

Older children and teenagers enjoy being read to as well. Of course, the content and style should be appropriate to their age. It may be that you read to these children from a short magazine article, a newspaper story, a passage from a good book, or from the family Bible during dinner. Teenagers might respond better to this when it is done in a spontaneous way. For example, during dinner conversation you could respond to a comment by saying, "Hey, that reminds me of something I read in the paper today . . ."

Having your child practice reading aloud is also a good exercise. She learns and practices public speaking skills by reading aloud. This is good to practice at home because most teachers in primary and middle school grades, and many teach-ers in high school, ask students to read aloud to the class. If your child can do this well, it will be a tremendous boost to her classroom confidence. As a classroom teacher, I saw many students who were embarrassed to read aloud in class largely due to a lack of practice.

There is a trick you can teach your child to help him read aloud smoothly and with greater confidence. He can train himself to move his eyes ahead of his mouth. Rather than looking at the word he is pronouncing when he is pronouncing it, he should look one to two words ahead of the word he is saying out loud. This will give his brain enough time to process the word he is looking at so he can link it to the other words in the sentence in a continuous stream rather than a halting fashion.

It will require some practice to do that with ease. At first it may cause him to read faster because his eye is moving ahead of his mouth. In time he will be able to pace himself. Not only will he be able to read more smoothly, but that split second of time will allow him to put the right emotion and emphasis in his voice while reading.

Encouraging Your Child to Demonstrate Mature Reading Skills

You can train your child to sharpen her reading skills. Developing reading skills takes practice, and you can help your child practice. Here are a few steps you can take:

Ask the teacher what reading skills your child should be mastering at his grade level. If your child is in junior or senior high school, you can get this information from his English teacher. Such information should be readily available to parents. The Indianapolis public school system, for instance, published an excellent guide, *What Reading Skills Must Your Child Master in Junior High School?*, which lists and describes eleven reading skills that parents can help foster in their teenagers.

Find out from the teacher what book or essay your child will be reading in the near future. Give yourself enough time to borrow a copy of the book from the teacher and read it yourself. If it is an entire book instead of a short story or essay, you can stay ahead of your child by one chapter. The teacher will be delighted that you are so involved with your child's learning!

At the time you get the book, ask the teacher what the intended learning outcome is. What skills will your child acquire, or what message will he receive? In short, what is your child supposed to learn from reading the material, and how will he be able to demonstrate his learning?

Before your child reads the material, talk with her about any new things she will learn. This will help her mentally prepare for and identify the learning when it occurs. If your child knows what she is supposed to learn before she reads the material, she will most likely learn it better when she reads it.

For instance, you may want your child to learn about expository writing (an informative piece as opposed to a story). Expository writing is generally used in textbooks. This book is an example of expository writing. It is important to understand that an exposition has a main idea and supporting points. Exposition has structure. It is not simply a set of facts strung together. If your child does not understand this, she lacks the skill to properly digest an author's message.

To help your child learn about what to look for in an exposition, you can talk about what it means to have a main idea and supporting ideas in a text. How does a reader identify the author's main idea? Where does a reader look for the author's supporting points? If you discuss these things before your child reads the material, she will know what to look for and will better understand the concept of expository writing.

Other skills that may be appropriate for your child to learn (depending on her age and ability) are:

- Using new vocabulary words.
- Understanding more complex sentence structure.
- Abilities to make inferences and evaluations.
- Abilities to combine what is read with her own experiences.
- Appreciation for how the author has written (understanding style, characterization, narrative, and plot).
- Ability to identify and understand various devices such as satire, humor, poetry, narrative, dialogue, and exposition.

Discuss the text with your child. This exercises the mind. Just as your child needs to exercise his physical muscles, so he also needs to exercise his mental muscles. Just as he learns to be coordinated in running, throwing a ball, jumping rope, or swinging a bat, so also he must acquire reading comprehension skills of inference, logic, objectivity, synthesis, evaluation, and appreciation. You can stretch your child's comprehension "muscles" by having him read a variety of material and discussing each passage. Just as you target specific muscles for development in physical exercise, so you can target specific comprehension skills for development. You can do that by asking your child specific questions that require him to summarize, evaluate, analyze, infer, show appreciation for the author's style, or synthesize the passage with other information he already knows.

Ellen, a mother of a middle-school student, told me she has made a routine of talking to her son about what he is reading. "I ask him several times a week what he is reading. He knows I'm going to want to discuss it, so he comes home prepared with good answers." And in the process she finds many opportunities to stretch her son's thinking skills.

Have your child write about what she has read. Writing about what she has read means she must deliberately think about its meaning. To put the author's message in her own words requires your child to digest it and reconstruct it in a similar way. This takes extra time, and you need to evaluate whether your child needs the additional work.

You can have your child write one paragraph about what he has read on a four-by-six-inch index card. At the top of each card, your child should write the name of the book and the chapter, section, or page numbers that are appropriate. He can also include the date he read it. Ask him to write a one-paragraph answer to one question or instruction such as:

- Summarize the story (if there is a story) or main idea (if the passage was informational).
- What did you like and dislike about the story?
- Which character did you like the most and why?
- What message do you think the author was trying to communicate through the story?

- Do you agree with the author's point? Why?
- Write about how what you read, in some way, relates to something that has happened in your life.
- Use one word to summarize the message of what you read, and explain why you chose that word.

That exercise will stretch your child's mental muscles. It will cause her to think in greater depth about what she has read. Let her read the question before she reads the passage. By reading the question first, she will engage in active reading—that is, she will be thinking about what she is reading, she will be asking herself questions, and she will be looking for answers. Discuss her answer for a few minutes.

Store the index cards in a box, and give her a tangible reward for the work. Younger children may need a reward for each card completed. Older children can wait to be rewarded after completing several cards.

Another excellent way to teach your child to think critically about what he is reading is to have him write double-entry journals. This is a very simple exercise, yet it can work well in stretching your child's mental muscles.

Have your child divide a piece of paper into two columns. At the top of the left-hand column have him write "Quotes" and at the top of the right-hand column have him write "My Thoughts." As he reads the book, article, or textbook he should write down any quotes that are interesting to him. The quotes can be as short as one word, a phrase, or a sentence. After the quote, he should put the page number where it is found in parentheses for referencing later if needed.

In the right-hand column, directly to the right of the quote he copied, he writes his thoughts about the quote. When he does this, he moves beyond merely reading the story to thinking about it and interacting with it. It is similar to writing in the margins of a book or underlining the text, but instead of marking up the book he is writing his thoughts on a separate piece of paper.

Younger children can benefit from a modified form of this activity. As your child reads a book, she can dictate to you an interesting quote and her thoughts. In this way she can learn, even as a young reader, to ask herself questions and think about what she is reading.

A Balanced Reading Diet

Maximizing your child's reading ability means having various reading materials available in your home for yourself and your child. The National Assessment of Educational Progress reports that students with exposure to newspapers, magazines, books, and encyclopedias at home tend to have greater reading skills.[3] Different reading materials use different writing styles and expand your child's skill at reading and comprehension. Newspapers most often use the classic question-answer format of who, what, when, where, and how in the first paragraph or two. The style is straightforward and to the point. Styles vary among magazines, and it is a good idea to subscribe to one for your child that matches both his interest and his reading level. Books offer the greatest variety of styles and subjects. Encyclopedias offer, in one place, the widest variety of information for your child.

Do not assume that your child is being exposed to a wide variety of material and the opportunity to read a great deal at school. Unfortunately, many students are asked to fill out worksheets requiring only literal comprehension skills. These students don't read for pleasure at school very much at all. This is changing, however. Many schools have begun to emphasize reading again, but you should check with your child's teacher to find out exactly the quantity and quality of reading your child does at school.

Just as you need a variety of foods to have a balanced meal, you need a variety of reading materials. A regular routine for reading is just as important as a regular routine for eating. The best time may be just before turning the lights out for bed. If you established a regular routine of reading a story to your child before bedtime when he was younger, it is a natural transition to have him read for himself when he is older.

But the time spent reading in bed should not be for homework. That should be done earlier in the day. Bedtime reading is for pleasure: a good novel, a magazine article, or the sports page of the newspaper. The time that you allow for this can vary according to the appropriateness for your child. As your child grows older, you can create an incentive to read by allowing him to stay up a few minutes longer if he is in bed reading.

It is important to emphasize reading for pleasure, since a majority of what a student reads is required reading for school. It is a job of sorts. Your child needs to realize that reading is not just for obtaining academic information but for enjoyment, as well. Reading touches us emotionally with laughter, sorrow, anger, or excitement. It can give us insight for personal growth or fascinate us with profound ideas. Reading can introduce us to other people and other cultures that we can enjoy as if we were there. A good novel can create a setting and characters so real that it transports the reader to that setting and, for the moment, becomes more real than the reader's own world. This is the magic you want your child to experience!

Using the Library Effectively

Knowing how to use the library effectively is to reading what shopping at the grocery store is to eating. If you can find the right foods, you can have delicious meals. If you can find the right books and materials, you can have delightful reading and an easier time with homework, as well. Here are a few guidelines for using your local library effectively:

1. *Go to the library on a regular basis.* A 1992 report by the National Center for Educational Statistics stated that students in grades four, eight, and twelve who used the library weekly or monthly had the highest reading abilities.[4] It did not comment on whether regular use of the library *contributed* to the higher reading levels or was a *result* of students who had better reading skills. It would, however, be reasonable to assume that making a habit of using the library as a family will have a positive impact on your child's comfort with reading. It will, at least, indicate that reading is a priority in your family.

2. *Become familiar with all that the library has to offer.*
Your local library is not just a storehouse for books.
It has back issues of magazines and reference materials such as almanacs, directories, and encyclopedias. Depending on its size, your library may have
specialized reference materials such as the *Dictionary of American History*, the *Encyclopedia of Education*, or the *International Encyclopedia of Statistics*.
Your library may have old newspapers stored on
microfilm. The *Readers Guide to Periodical Literature*
is an excellent source for finding magazine articles
listed by subjects.

Go to your local library on a day when there are
not too many people there, and ask the librarian to
explain the major resources at your disposal. Also,
ask the librarian about special events the library
might sponsor such as summer reading programs.

3. *Practice using a variety of library sources.* Teach your
child how to use the library services by doing a
scavenger hunt. Go to the library without your child,
and create a list of ten things he will be able to find
there. The ten items should require him to use a
variety of sources, ranging from books to encyclopedias and from periodical guides to computer-based
card catalogs. For instance, you can have him write
down the title of the book with the call number
768.249 or the name of the 1988 magazine article on
submarines written by Jack Walters.

The level of scavenging difficulty needs to be
geared to your child's age and ability level. Reward
him with a prize for successfully completing the
hunt. Of course, just as the level of difficulty should
be geared to his age, so the reward should be too.
Take along several of your child's friends, and make
it a cooperative group game or a good-natured compe-
tition. For instance, have them successfully complete
the hunt before they have a pizza party at your house.

A Word About Rewards

You may feel uncomfortable about giving a tangible reward to your child for academic achievement. After all, isn't a child supposed to learn to be internally motivated to succeed in school? Aren't rewards only a gimmick to motivate him to do what he is supposed to do on his own? The answer is that we all work for rewards, and there is nothing wrong with them, though you certainly don't have to use them.

A reward can be as simple as a pat on the back, a word of appreciation, or an approving smile. Intangible rewards of appreciation and recognition are vitally important. They help us develop an understanding of what we are capable of doing. Intangible rewards help us handle failures without feeling that we are failures. They give us internal strength.

However, tangible rewards are important too. If you do not believe that, go to your boss tomorrow and tell him you only want a pat on the back at the end of the week instead of a paycheck. Of course, you wouldn't do that!

A few years ago, a mother contacted me for help because her son hated to read. He was in first grade and was well behind his classmates. Each time she tried to read to him, he threw a temper tantrum. If she tried to get him to read aloud, he would whine. I asked her if there was anything that aroused his enthusiasm. "Yes," she said. "He is crazy about collecting stickers." The mother set up a system of rewards: one sticker for each page he read, even if the page only had one sentence on it. A few months later, she reported that the reward system worked. Everyday *he* initiated reading aloud to her. She proudly told me, "He has already read 500 pages!"

Four years later, I had the opportunity of visiting with that mother. Her son was in the fifth grade. "Does he still struggle with reading?" I asked.

"Not at all," she said. "He loves to read!"

"Do you still have to reward him?"

"No. He grew out of needing a reward once he learned how rewarding it was to read well," she told me.

A simple grade is often too abstract a reward for a child. Your child may not be motivated to push to increase his grade from a B to an A. Some children don't see what the big deal is about grades as long as they are passing the class. In those cases, it is better to have the added incentive of a tangible reward. Your reward system needs to be reasonable, fair, and consistent. Plan ahead for the time when your child gets his motivational juices flowing and exceeds your wildest expectations. Will you be able to remain consistent with the reward, or will you change the system because it is getting too expensive? If you change the rules in the middle of the game, your child will feel cheated. Create a system that gives your child incentive from the start and that you can afford to maintain to the end.

Many parents give financial allowances to their children for doing household chores. Why not tie the money to reaching levels of excellence in homework? Money is a tangible reward to which every child can relate. Be creative in your system: a penny for every page your child reads; a dollar for an A he receives on a homework assignment (less for younger children); twenty dollars for every A as a final grade for each class, ten dollars for every grade of B. Come up with your own system—whatever works for you and your child.

Summary

Maximizing reading skills means more than simply being able to pronounce the words on the page. Your child must be constantly developing his thinking skills too. You can help him do this by knowing what kinds of skills he should be developing at each grade level and explaining to him how to practice those skills.

If you have a wide variety of reading material and set a good example of reading yourself, you will increase your child's interest in reading. You can increase your child's reading proficiency by creating fun, skill-building activities for him. These activities include going to the library, having your child write about what he reads, and keeping a double-entry journal of his reading.

In the next chapter you will learn how too much television can undermine your child's reading and academic success.

8
Limit Television

Parent Power Tool #6: Monitor the Amount of
Television You Watch

Your Goal
*The television is on for less than one hour each day or seven
hours each week. When we watch it, we converse about the
story or information shown. I feel that we have broken the
TV-viewing habit.*

It would be easy to write about how terrible television is.
It's an easy target. But I struggled with this chapter because I
like to watch television too. My research on the subject as well
as my experience of seeing TV's effect on students causes me
to view television fairly negatively. Still, I have to admit I enjoy
it. Television has forever changed how we receive information
and how we entertain ourselves. The challenge is to find a
balance with it in our lives. The key is to handle it responsibly.

You and your children cannot escape the television because
it permeates our culture. Even families who have gotten rid of
their television set have not eliminated it completely from
their lives. Their children are bound to see it on occasion. And
even if you never watch it, TV affects aspects of our culture
from fashion to politics. For all the criticism we heap on the
"boob tube" there *are* advantages to television.

- Certain events are best seen on TV. The inauguration
  of a president, the Olympics, a local sports event that
  is sold out, or a breaking news story are just a few
  events that you most likely would not see if it were not
  for TV.
- It exposes us to faraway locations, and it enhances our
  understanding of the world. Travel documentaries,
  international news events, and even movies can enhance our awareness of the world.

- It can fill gaps in our learning. For instance, we might not want to struggle through one of Shakespeare's plays, but we can see it on television. Granted, we miss the beauty and challenge of his writing, but we still can be moved by the message in his drama.
- It rapidly delivers the daily news to us.
- It warns us of consumer issues related to our health and safety.
- It entertains us and helps us escape, for a time, the stresses of life.
- It raises political and social issues that cause us to think.
- It creates a sense of national community by making us more familiar with the lives of Americans living in different parts of the country.
- It introduces us to products and services that enhance our lives.

It would be rash to conclude that *all* television is useless or harmful. What is harmful is the amount of television we watch. We have become addicted to this plug-in drug, and that addiction has consequences.

Television affects your child in three major ways: by its content, by its distraction from life, and by its conditioning. In this chapter, I will focus on those three issues and show you how to help your child watch television responsibly.

Addicted to Television

The average child between the ages of six and eleven watches more than 3.5 hours of television each day.[1] Multiply this by 365 days in a year to get 1,277.5 hours. Divide that by the fourteen waking hours a child has each day, and you arrive at the fact that just over ninety-one days each year of a child's life is devoted exclusively to viewing television! Between the ages of six and eleven a child spends more than 547 days or one and a half years of his little life watching television!

If we extend those figures throughout a person's life (which is justified since some calculations show the average American spending as much as 4.5 hours watching TV each day) to age seventy-five, we find that person has spent 16.5 years in front of the television. What do we have to show for those 16.5 years of devotion? Certainly you will have received information that enriches your life. You will have learned, to some degree, about the world and about politics, about nature and about new products and services. A consumer report might have alerted you to a harmful or fraudulent product. But do those examples justify the equivalent of more than sixteen years of continuous viewing?

The most immediate danger to your child is not only some of the messages he receives from television programming but also the time he wastes in inactivity while watching it. You might recoil in horror to think of your child being fed one and a half years of Hollywood's values through the television set, but you should be more shocked to think of your child sitting motionless, staring at a box for that long. While he is inside watching television, he is not outside playing a game or exploring his world or talking with Mom and Dad. When he grows older, he is not doing his homework or reading a book or working at a hobby or interacting with the family.

One mother who helped her children break the addiction of television told me, "I feel like I've saved my children so much time. They do so much more now."

Here are some television diet tips:

1. Keep your children outdoors as much as possible. Get them skates, bicycles, hockey sticks, baseball equipment, or whatever they may need to facilitate an active outdoor playtime.
2. Once a week or every few days, go through the TV guide with your children and together select the programs they will watch. This avoids grazing through the channels in search of something to watch. Using the TV then becomes a deliberate

rather than habitual act. If you are wondering how much television to allow each week, one elementary school principal suggested to me that he would like to see students watch no more than thirty minutes of television each night.

3. Videotape programs (with the TV turned off), and watch them after homework or other activities are completed. This will also allow you to space out the viewing time over the week when favorite programs appear on the same day.

4. Make a game of eliminating all TV viewing for one week. Challenge your children with a reward if they can discipline themselves not to watch any TV during that time. If you do this once a month, it is like adding twenty-one days to your year!

5. Turn the TV off during times of family interaction or when the children are playing. Don't use it as background noise.

Television Learning

If your children are like most in America, they suffer from the effects of television viewing. They watch too much; they are negatively influenced by what they see; their schoolwork suffers because of their attention to television.

You may even feel that in your home the television set has replaced you as leader. Your television dictates that your family schedules conform to its programming schedules. It tells your children how much effort to put into their homework. (Hurry up! Rush through it! I'm about to start your favorite program.) It demands that family conversation stop while it speaks. It won't allow anyone to ask it questions, and it seems to be an authority on everything.

A major problem of learning by television is that the message evaporates into oral history never to be repeated, never to be reread for analysis or pondering. The person on the program may voice an important and insightful thought, but it is lost in thin air as the program moves to the next attention-catching scene.

A book, on the other hand, can be read repeatedly. The reader can stop and ponder an important sentence. He can go back a few pages to an assertion the author made previously and compare it with the passage he is currently reading. Reading is self-paced and allows the reader to think deeply as he is reading. Television follows the slogan, "The show must go on," and keeps the pace moving rapidly. Thinking is not as important as reacting. One reason television is so much more popular with children than homework is that television watching is easier to do. Reacting is always easier than thinking.

Educational psychologist Dr. Jane Healy, in her book *Endangered Minds,* warns that television may actually physically alter a child's brain. She suggests that television's visual and auditory stimuli create patterns in the brain's neurological connections that are different (and inferior for learning) than those created by the act of reading.

> Children's brains develop connections within and between areas, depending on the type of exercise they get. A good brain for learning develops strong and widespread neural highways that can quickly and efficiently assign different aspects of a task to the most efficient system. Such a brain is able to talk to itself, instantly sending messages from one area to another. Such efficiency is developed only by active practice in thinking and learning which, in turn, builds increasingly stronger connections. A growing suspicion among brain researchers is that extensive television viewing may affect development of these kinds of connections. It may also induce habits of using the wrong systems for various types of learning.[2]

Just as we condition and tone our bodies through a healthy diet and appropriate exercise, so our minds are shaped by our mental diet and exercise. While television viewing is a passive activity, that does not mean it does not affect your child's habits of mind. No matter what the content of the program is, your child is being shaped by the medium as well as by the message. It is essential, then, that your child receive a balanced diet of mental stimulation that includes rigorous challenges to his thinking skills.

What About *Sesame Street*?

Sesame Street borrows heavily from commercial techniques: short, repetitive messages, lots of action, an emphasis on fun, and little that challenges the viewer to think.

As a specialist in children's educational development, Healy evaluated *Sesame Street*'s educational worth and concluded, "The worst thing about *Sesame Street* is that people believe it is educationally valuable.... When we encourage preschoolers to watch *Sesame Street*, we are programing them to enjoy—and perhaps even need—overstimulation, manipulation, and neural habits that are antagonistic to academic learning."[3] In her critique of the program, she cites that, contrary to popular opinion, the show does not significantly help vocabulary development; it distorts print media; it offers up bits of information as education rather than larger bites of meaningful education given in a broader context; it undermines the child's ability to be a good listener and pay attention in class; and it overstimulates the child's comprehension abilities and causes the child's brain to stop thinking. Children's television can be an entertaining diversion, but as an important educational tool it falls short. I have listed a few ways to help your child think while he watches the TV.

Television Viewing Tips
That Enhance Learning

1. Avoid depending on television as a baby-sitter. Occupy your children's time with more engaging and self-directed activities. It is better for them to do something rather than passively watch others do it.
2. Help your child use the skill of evaluation by asking her what she thinks of a show she just watched. Did she like it or dislike it and why?

3. Mute the television during commercials, and ask your child what he thinks is going to happen next in the story. Make a game of seeing who guesses most correctly. Learning requires active thinking and making meaning from information. A few questions while watching can help do this with a television program.
4. Help your child develop the thinking skill of comparison by asking him to compare one show with another or one character with another in the same show or an entirely different show.
5. Although TV can dull creativity and imagination, you can counter that effect by asking your child how she would have changed the plot to create a different ending.
6. Help your child with the skill of summarization by asking him to tell you the highlights of a show he watched.
7. Help your child develop his analytical skills by asking how he thinks the production techniques of the show affected the telling of the story. For instance, ask him how such things as camera zooms, quick edits, and mood music helped tell the story. Watch a show with the sound turned down for a few minutes and note the difference it has on the story.
8. Help your children see that a TV show gives only one perspective on a subject and that there are others to consider. Talk about the message of the show and whether you agree with it.
9. Follow up a show that is set in a foreign country by looking up the location with your child in an atlas or on the globe.

Television Content

As television programs compete for audience attention, they push the boundaries of decency in order to be noticed. Programmers appeal to our lower natures because they know we are drawn to the forbidden, indulgent, and sinful. Our sins are lived vicariously through the television characters. Yet these television programs are entertaining. When I write that they are entertaining, I wonder how my definition of entertainment has become so warped. Television's appeal often creates a struggle between my lower nature and the refining sensibilities my parents worked so hard to give me.

James B. Twitchell observes in his book *Carnival Culture: The Trashing of Taste in America* that most of what is on television is vulgar, crude, and tasteless. His concern is that by engulfing ourselves in a daily bath of vulgarity, we lose our ability to appreciate what is truly beautiful. Our ability to discern the graceful from the garish or the humorous from the crude will be lost. He comments that when we no longer classify certain entertainments as vulgar, we will also be unable to classify their opposites as art. [4] We become culturally numb.

Programs that assault our sensibilities are glowingly described as bold and daring. After years of television viewing, I learn to value celebrity over significance, entertainment over learning, image over substance, and passion over reason. Television entertainment blasts us with a continual barrage of fads, freaks, and folly—and we love it.

Even with more substantive programs, such as documentaries or news programs, we need to think carefully while we watch, because television shapes our view of what is important. For instance, journalist Stephan Lesher, in his book *Media Unbound*, points out:

By the end of the 1970s, three out of every four Americans learned most of their news from television. Every second American received all his or her news from television.

By 1980, whether the subject was Vietnam, black militancy, student rage, Watergate, Iran, Abscam, assassination attempts or presidential primaries and elections, it could be argued that, to an extraordinary degree, until television reported it, it had not happened. [5]

This nonexistent-unless-televised concept gives rise to events staged only for media attention. Press conferences, publicity stunts, political campaigns, and most protests live and die by whether television cameras show up. They are not real events in the sense that they would not happen unless television cameras were present. Television requires that the message be dramatic, captivating, and most of all, visual. Only those messages that can be packaged in that format can be delivered and, thus, heard.

Take, for example, the sound bite that dominates political coverage today. In the 1960s, the average length of a television sound bite was forty-five seconds. Today it has been shortened to ten seconds. Contrary to popular opinion, this is not the candidates' fault. The event (a speech, debate, or interview) is shaped by the medium of communication. The rapid pace required to hold viewer's attention demands that speakers use quick, catchy slogans rather than lengthy expositions on their political positions. In other words, an idea that cannot be expressed within two or three sentences is no longer an idea that can be communicated. The format of television has, by its nature, determined what ideas will be heard.

I have found this to be true in my own experience. A few years ago I was asked to appear on the morning talk show *CBS This Morning* to debate an educational issue. We were given a five-minute time slot for the segment, which I was told was considerable (they originally gave us only three minutes). Before the program, I calculated that if there were three people talking during the segment—the host, myself, and my opponent—and there were only three questions asked and responded to by both sides, my total time to respond to each question would be thirty seconds. I overestimated. In reviewing the videotape of the segment, I found that my three responses lasted twenty, fifteen, and thirty seconds. In this environment, the best I could hope for was to make a few poignant statements that left the viewer with a better impression of my position than that of my opponents. That is not dialogue; that is sloganeering dressed up to look like serious information.

Making an impression is the aim of most television programs. Brigtta Hoijer, in her study "Television-Evoked Thoughts and Their Relation to Comprehension," found that the comprehension and recall levels of people who watch television news is very low.[6] We watch the news but often cannot even repeat what we just saw. The news has become just another form of entertainment. Television producers recognize the entertainment value of news, and news stories have become more and more dramatically presented. A new genre of tabloid news has sprung up that openly acknowledges and accentuates the drama.

Tips for Dealing with Television Content

1. Become familiar with what TV shows your children watch, and make sure the shows express values you want your children to learn.

2. When a program has a good moral theme, you can reinforce the moral with a comment or two. Your comments don't have to be lengthy lectures but can be brief observations such as, "It's really true what Tim and Sally said: It's not good to fight and argue with each other ...," or, "I like how Mr. Smith ended up treating his neighbor right because ..."

3. Don't let the TV be the only input your children receive on matters of art, music, and taste. Teach your children what you consider to be beautiful, inspiring, and in good taste.

4. Help your older children to be discerning regarding the message they receive in commercials, news reports, and shows. Help them see what is *not* being said about a subject as well as any bias that you see affecting what *is* being said. You can help yourself do this by subscribing to conservative or Christian magazines or newsletters that are outside the mainstream media and offer a perspective other than network programming.

Television's Conditioning of Your Child

The consequence of your child's shifting away from reading toward television viewing is his being conditioned to favor imagery over logic, narrative (story) over exposition (explanation), immediacy over pondering, and entertainment over thoughtfulness. When children go to school having been thus conditioned, they struggle to pay attention in class because they can focus for only short periods of time. They struggle to think perceptively about a subject since they are used to having conclusions and interpretations delivered to them. They struggle with sticking to a learning task that is not particularly entertaining because television never lets them be bored.

The language of television is geared for about the fourth-grade level. Worse than that, television combats such essential learning skills as the ability to plan, sequence, organize, and classify ideas. All those thinking processes are already done for your child and delivered to him in the program.

Television allows us to jump immediately from viewing to responding (feeling). Reading, on the other hand, requires an interpretative stage. We read the content, interpret the author's meaning, evaluate it, relate it to our experience, and then respond to it. Television viewing skips these thinking steps. For example, think of any number of television commercials. Rarely will you find a commercial that states a naked proposition and appeals to your reason. A majority of commercials appeal to an emotion and create a desire in the viewer to act. The viewer jumps from viewing to acting or at least to desiring to act.

Jill, a mother of twins, told me, "We really noticed that when we stopped watching so much television our children's level of greed went down dramatically. During Christmas, they hardly knew what they wanted because their lust to have things hadn't been stirred up by the commercials."

In hours of watching television, we condition ourselves to suspend rational judgment and thinking. By the time the average child enters first grade, he has watched more than sixty thousand commercials, which teach him to stop thinking and start responding emotionally.

This goal of creating an emotional response in the viewer causes a student to elevate his emotions above his reason regarding his academic studies. Thus conditioned, it is not so important to him what he *thinks* about his studies but what he *feels* about them. His feelings rather than his thoughts become the basis of his judgments because he has spent thousands of hours being trained to think with his heart, not with his head.

Television Viewing Tips

1. Mute the TV during commercials to reduce distractions from the story and lessen the temptation to want what the commercial is selling.
2. Teach your child to critically analyze the message of the commercial. (This will be more successful with older children.) Help him make a habit of questioning if the message is true, if the product will really give him the benefit it claims, and if he truly needs it. Help him discern if the advertiser is using the classic marketing technique of selling the sizzle or selling the steak.
3. Make a habit of turning off the TV as soon as the last scene of the TV show has faded to black. This will allow you and your child to reflect on the message of the program without the distraction of commercials. Interact for a minute or two with your child about the programs message. This can be simple, such as comments like:

   "That was really funny. I liked it when . . ." or,
   "I didn't like that one character who . . ." or,
   "Wow! That really made me think about. . . ."

If You Want to Dump the TV

One teacher explained to me what he tells new parents: "When the baby comes home from the hospital, the television should go out the door." Frankly, that is too drastic for most of us. Although we complain about the TV, in all honesty, we don't want to completely eliminate it from our lives. However, if you do want to take this commendable step, there are some things to keep in mind.

If your child hasn't lived without a television, it may be hard for him to imagine what it would be like. The difficulty is not just in missing the entertainment, but in feeling disconnected from the world.

If your child abruptly stops watching television altogether, he may experience an initial sense of isolation from the world. The feeling can be somewhat unnerving for the television addict. Boredom may soon follow the feeling of isolation.

Sarah and Kevin, the parents of six boys, have lived without television in the house for the past two years. "We definitely went through withdrawals," she told me. "It seemed too quiet around the house. The boys were bored and moped around the house. I felt like a camp activities director for a while, helping them come up with other things to do. But it wasn't long before they began initiating activities."

Here is a list of alternatives to watching television that you can suggest to your children:

- Sports
- Hobbies
- Homework
- Family walks
- Play board games
- Shop
- Read a book
- Learn a musical instrument
- Write to a pen pal
- Interact with the family
- Cook something fun

To successfully remove the television set, it is a good idea to plan alternate activities in advance. Create a schedule of activities starting from the time your child comes home from school to the time he goes to bed. The schedule doesn't have to be followed as if you are in the army, but it will help you to answer the age-old question from a child, "I'm bored. What do I do now?" At first your child may react in disbelief to the notion that you expect him to do something with his time other than watch television. But within a short time, he will adjust to the new TV-free diet, and his innate creativity will begin to blossom once again.

"We sat the children down and told them how we felt about what the TV was doing to our family," Sarah explained. "They understood and didn't seem to mind very much, especially when they knew that we would be suffering right along with them."

Getting rid of the television doesn't mean you have to prohibit your children from ever watching it. If they are at a friend's house and their homework is done, you might allow them, on occasion, to watch a good program. One dad I know who got rid of the television in his family takes his son to the pizza parlor to watch football games. He makes it a special father-son activity.

The goal is to break the *habit* of watching television. Totally restricting your children from ever watching television under any circumstances may be an impossible and unreasonable goal. Handling the television responsibly is a tremendous Parent Power Tool! I am convinced that when you implement even a few of the strategies outlined in this chapter your children will be freed up to do better work in school.

Summary

Television can be a powerful force in shaping what your child thinks about and the way she actually thinks. Unfortunately, the way television encourages your child to interact with information is the opposite of the habits she needs for the classroom. Whereas television stresses emotion, immediacy, and entertainment, school work requires reason, reflection, and self-discipline.

It is imperative that you restrict and monitor what your child watches or eliminate the television set altogether. When you limit viewing time, you are putting the TV in its proper place— as a storyteller, not an extra family member.

It is hard to imagine that allowing yourself a few minutes of mindless distraction will cause great harm (unless the images you view are of the vulgar sort that make a negative imprint on your memory).The danger of television is that it appeals to our tendency toward laziness and titillation. When we indulge our children's desire for this mind candy too much, there is no question we are diluting a proper nutritional diet for their minds. *Every hour you reduce your television viewing each day is like adding over twenty-six (fourteen-hour) days to your year.* In that time, your child can master an academic skill, develop a hobby, or build better relationships with family and friends.

Replacing the TV with conversations is one way of challenging your children's thinking skills. In the next chapter you will discover exactly how to use your conversations to boost their thinking skills and help them in school.

9
Promote Thinking

Parent Power Tool #7: Promote Thinking
Skills Through Conversation

Your Goal
*We have prolonged conversations about what is happening
in our lives each day. We talk about problems and successes.
We ask each other stimulating questions, make appropriate
comments, share our own experiences, and listen well to
each other.*

I get excited when I think about how this chapter can help
your child develop his thinking, and I hope that, as you read,
you get excited too! With the techniques outlined here, your
child can become a sharper thinker.

You have good reason to be concerned that your child may
not automatically learn to think in the demanding ways necessary for problem solving, job skills, college success, political
involvement, or simply formulating and expressing his ideas
and values. The force of pop culture conditions him to feel and
react rather than reason and respond thoughtfully. What you
may not know is that you have a tool right at your fingertips—
or more appropriately, at the tip of your tongue—to enhance
your child's thinking ability: conversation.

A lot of people overlook conversation as a tool for helping
their children in school because they see it as commonplace.
We all talk every day. We talk in order to find out something
or direct someone to do something, but we often don't think
about how the talk itself creates foundations for greater academic accomplishment.

The way you interact verbally with your child at home can
have a profound impact on her skills in school. You may think
that the amount of conversation with a teacher at school
outweighs dialogue at home. However, one study found that,
at home, 78 percent of conversations were between child and

parent whereas only 21 percent were between children. At school those percentages were reversed. Only 28 percent of the conversations moved from child to teacher, whereas 72 percent were between children.[1] The teacher has the entire class to be concerned with, and her communication is more of a monologue than a dialogue. There are fewer people at home, so children have greater interaction with adults there. Children and teenagers benefit a great deal from talking with adults who have more experience in challenging conversational techniques.

One parent explained to me an unusual way she found to promote conversation. "This may sound comical," she wrote, "but having only one car in our family has promoted conversation. Every day we are forced to talk to each other to make arrangements, and we are forced to think of the needs of others in our family. Having to take each other places gives us more time to talk."

As you think about your family conversations, the question you should ask yourself is whether the conversations you have with your child or teenager are the kind that enhance thinking ability. Research has been done to suggest that a good foundation in oral language is important to a child's familiarity with written language. Dr. Jane Healy refers to a "firm base of oral language skills" as being essential for good writing and analytical thinking.[2] A relationship exists between your ability to think and the types of conversations you engage in.

What Does It Mean to Think?

Thinking means the ability to direct your thoughts in a mental task. Professor Vincent Ruggiero, a pioneer in the field of thinking skills instruction, refers to this type of thinking as "purposeful mental activity over which a person exercises some control."[3]

It may seem odd to you that your child's school talks about teaching thinking skills. After all, hasn't education always been about learning to think? The answer is both yes and no. Your child's mind is always thinking in the sense that it is trying to find order in his experience. Education moves beyond this continual consciousness and attempts to impose greater order and concepts on his world. He learns to refine his ability to analyze, evaluate, question, monitor, and plan.

What many educators mean when they refer to thinking skills is what researchers call metacognition—thinking about thinking. This is a deliberate act of consciously using a variety of mental techniques. The teacher may instruct your child to write a report. Certainly many thinking-skills activities are involved in writing a report. Your child must choose a main point and support it with subpoints, analyze various sources, evaluate and select the best material to use, order it in a logical sequence, and write his thoughts down in a way that makes sense for the reader. However, though the teacher may teach each step in the process (go to the library, select material on your subject, write a one-page report), she may not overtly teach the deliberate thinking skills involved in each step (analyze, categorize, evaluate, sequence). If she doesn't, you can.

Thoughtful conversations at home can promote deliberate mental activity. In fact, your home makes a wonderful laboratory for teaching thinking. You and your child can engage in solving real-life problems together using conversation. For example, you may be planting flowers in your yard. How should you arrange them? By color? By size? By type of flower? How far apart should you plant them? How deep should you bury the roots? You can either direct your child to complete the task a certain way, or you can discuss with him the various alternatives and help him practice thinking.

Another example might be in how you order your weekend. You want to accomplish several things in the two days: household chores, errands around town, a visit with friends, your child's sports activity, church, and playing a family game. You can schedule these activities by categorizing them according to proximity to your house (do the things in the house first and the things closest to the house next). You can schedule them around the events that have fixed times, such as the soccer game and church. If you bring your child into the decision-making process through conversation, you are giving him practice in a variety of thinking skills.

When you do this, explain which thinking skill is involved. For example, if he is helping you sort the clean laundry, you can define the problem—the clothes need to be sorted so each person gets the right clothing for the right dresser drawer—and have him practice categorizing. Explain to him that he will be using a thinking skill called categorizing which requires him to group things together based on what they have in common. He will have categories and subcategories: one for each family member and one for each type of clothing under each family member's group.

It is a good idea to have your child verbalize the thinking process by selecting a piece of clothing and asking himself out loud, "What category does this fit?" His verbalization will highlight the thinking skill in his mind. Later, when he is proficient at categorization, he will not need to verbalize his thoughts, but he will still mentally ask himself the same thinking-skills question.

Conversation and Thinking Skills

Good conversation promotes good thinking. To be a good conversationalist, your child must learn to listen to what others say. He must be able to analyze their ideas and compare them to his existing frame of reference. His mind must categorize the topic being discussed, sort through his memory on things that relate to the topic, and select appropriate information to add to the topic of conversation. He must differentiate between the main idea and distracting details that, though related to the subject, prevent the conversation from moving along. To express himself in conversation, he must be able to clarify his thoughts and present them in an orderly fashion, which requires logic or persuasion or insight.

To be a good conversationalist, the child must concentrate on the verbal exchanges that occur. He must focus and sustain his attention on what the other person is saying. He must understand the subtext—that is, the implied meaning of the speaker. What the speaker says may be true, but what he implies may be false. For instance, it may be a fact that John broke up with his girlfriend, Sally. The speaker, through facial expression and tone, may imply the opinion that the break up was a bad thing when, upon more careful examination, it could be judged to be a healthy decision.

A good conversationalist must be empathetic. That means placing himself in the speaker's position and feeling what he feels about a situation or idea. It requires a certain objectivity to understand the other person's viewpoint and emotions. This means that the hearer suspends judgment until the speaker is finished. That allows for a fair analysis of what the speaker says and means. Too often in conversations, party A is only half-listening to party B. While party B is talking, party A is busy thinking about what he is going to say next. That is not empathetic listening.

You can help your child develop good thinking skills through conversation by having extended dialogue that allows for probing of a subject. If your conversations frequently jump from one subject to another without requiring your child to sustain a line of reasoning, his thinking skills will not develop as well as they could.

The Art of Conversation

Eighteenth-century satirist Samuel Johnson once said, "Language is the dress of thought." If that is true, many of today's young people are practically naked. They (along with many adults) replace precise expression of their ideas with phrases such as "You know," "like," "I mean," "et cetera," and "sort of." These phrases are often cover for lack of clear thinking. "You know" generally means "Help me out here. I'm not sure how to say this." The term *et cetera* is acceptable to use in conversation. However, often when we use it we really mean, "I can't think of any other things to list in this category, but I want to sound like I know more than I do."

The annoying use of *like*, so common among young people today, generally has no connection with the thought at all and is verbal filler. On the other hand, it may be that the word *like* pops up in conversation so frequently because it generalizes the speakers thought. For instance, a teenager may state, "Roger was, like, 'Sure, you can use my car,'" and may be correctly expressing the thought that Roger said something similar to "Sure, you can use my car." But did the teenager truly mean to generalize, or is the statement a direct quote? And did the teenager mean to convey what Roger said or his state of being ("Roger was...")? The point is that, though this communicates effectively, it lacks precision.

Conversational Parts

If you reflect on your conversations you will notice that good conversations are a combination of four basic elements: telling about experiences, making comments, asking questions, and listening. Within these four elements lie the ingredients for helping your child develop his thinking skills. Let's take a look at each one.

Telling About Experiences

Conversation often involves telling others about your experiences. You and your child will have many conversations about things you have done separately and together. Telling about experiences requires your child to actively use his memory. He will also learn to categorize those details that support the main idea and enhance the story, versus those that, though part of the actual experience, are distracting.

You may have listened to your young child rambling on, recalling every detail of his story. If your child needs help sticking to the main point of his story, you can ask him to highlight the main parts. Tell him specifically that you want him to learn to summarize his story. A student learns best when the teacher explains what he is supposed to be learning from a given activity. The student, then, becomes an active learner and can recognize more readily when he has achieved the objective. By explaining to your child that you want him to learn to summarize things and by showing him how to do it, you will help him learn to think consciously. He will learn how to think about thinking.

Making Comments

A conversation is not a monologue—it requires the verbal exchange of at least two people. That means that each party must make appropriate comments that enhance the conversation. Your child or teenager can develop thinking skills better when you expand on and extend a topic he talks about. If he brings up a subject, you can extend the conversation by making comments on the topic. What do you think about the topic? Have you recently read something about it that you can add to the conversation? It is important to make comments that enhance rather than hinder the conversation. Condescending remarks, put-downs, or other negative comments are conversation inhibitors. Your child takes a risk when he converses with you. He exposes his thoughts to you. Will you accept them as worthy of discussion or reject them as trivial?

Helpful comments in conversations include: (1) something you read about the topic, (2) related news on the topic, (3) your thoughts or feelings about the topic, or (4) something you heard someone else say about the topic. Another important type of comment you can make is an encouraging remark. That signals to your child that you are pleased with his thinking. Such comments include statements such as: "Good idea!" "I'm glad you brought that up," and "Please go on." Those types of comments will encourage your child to have more conversations with you in the future.

Asking Questions

Questions are to conversations what keys are to doors—they turn walls into passageways. Questions open up conversations and keep them lively and moving. It is important that your child know how to both ask and answer thoughtful questions. Students who know how to do this are better able to handle the requirements of school successfully. They ask more questions in class and, thus, get more attention from the teacher and more help in their learning.

You and your child need to consciously think about how and when to use questions, as a painter thinks about how and when to use a certain paint brush. There are:

Questions that ask for elaboration:
   Could you give me an example?
   Is there more I need to know about this?
Questions that ask for clarification:
   How does that work?
   Do you mean to say . . . ?
   How is that different from . . . ?
   Why do you say that?
Questions that challenge:
   Do you really believe that?
   How could that be so?
Questions that seek evidence:
   What do you have to back up your assertion?
   Where did you hear that?
Questions about the relevance of a statement:
   So what?
   How is that related?
   Could you explain the connection?

Those are just a few of the many types of questions you can ask of your child and he can ask of you or his teacher. There are questions that fall into each category of thinking: contrasting, comparing, analyzing, evaluating, deciphering fact from opinion, clarifying cause and effect, following directions, discerning bias and propaganda, synthesizing ideas, applying what is stated, problem solving, and summarizing.

As he would select the right key to open the door in front of him, your child must learn to select the right question in class or while doing his homework to unlock his understanding of a particular subject. You can help your child learn to ask and answer questions by practicing them in conversation. Be overt about telling him, for instance, that you want him to practice asking questions that compare two things. For example, ask him how two of his friends are alike, how two of his classes are alike, or how one homework assignment is like another. I've listed some examples of the types of questions that target specific thinking skills.

Category of Thinking	Question
Comparison	How is x similar to y?
Contrast	How is x different from y?
Synthesis	What happens if we bring x and y together?
Evaluation	Is it good (or useful or correct)?
Fact versus opinion	Can I verify this information?
Cause and effect	What happened and why did it happen?
Following directions	What do I do next?
Discerning bias	What factors may warp a true picture of x?
Application	How does this work in the real world?
Problem solving	What are possible solutions?
Summarization	What are the main points to remember?

Asking those types of questions while listening is known as active listening. When your child does this, he is aggressively interacting with the information he hears. You can help him learn to have an inquisitive mind, which naturally asks insightful questions. When you have conversations that use a full range of questions, you are demonstrating for your child (and allowing him to practice) an important part of active thinking.

You may want to teach your child each category of thinking. Explain to him, for instance, what it means to compare two items. Teach him the question used to do comparisons. Then, give him ample opportunities to practice asking the comparison question in real-world settings. For example, have him compare two products in a grocery store. Even if the products are very different, looking for similarities will cause him to stretch his mental muscles to find comparisons.

Listening

"Conversation is two-way," a mother of two children told me, "so we find it important to listen, listen, listen to our kids. Some of the most profound conversations have occurred when we least expected it—on the way to the grocery store, getting ready for bed, setting the table, etc. This means spending time with our kids and picking up on opportunities when they are present, even if it's inconvenient."

One of the most important skills of being a good conversationalist is being a good listener. This requires an attitude of humility—you are not the only person worth hearing. A good listener suspends his desire to respond immediately to what the speaker is saying until the speaker is done. The most important thing to a good listener is accurately hearing what the other person said. Often students make mistakes on homework assignments because they did not listen well enough to the teacher's instructions. When your child practices good listening skills, he will not only follow directions better, but he will do better in other academic skills as well.

Your child can learn to be a good listener by practicing the four key elements of listening:

H *Honor* the person who is speaking.
E Make *Eye contact* with the speaker.
A *Ask* yourself questions about what the speaker is saying.
R *Respond* to what the speaker said (mentally or verbally).

Honor. To honor the other person means to show her respect. One of the best ways to show respect for another person is to listen to her. We have all experienced the rudeness of someone who does not really listen to us while we talk. For instance, at social gatherings, you know what you are sayng isn't being heard when the other person is looking over your shoulder and scanning the crowd for the next person he can talk to. The offending person is not listening to you, and the frustrated feeling you experience in that moment may be because you sense a slight loss of respect.

Eye contact. Making eye contact is important when listening. It helps focus your attention on the speaker, and it conveys to the speaker that you are listening. It is, however, possible to be looking at someone while not paying attention to what she is saying. For that reason you need to add the next part of listening: asking questions.

Ask. Mentally asking questions about what the speaker is saying helps focus your attention. A very simple question you can ask yourself while listening is, "What is he saying?" That is active listening. It requires that you analyze what is being said, focus on the important points, sort nonessential from essential information, seek logical connections, synthesize what you are hearing with what you already know, and evaluate the content and tone of what is being said.

Good listening is a learned skill. It is more than simply hearing what someone else is saying. It requires concentration. In *Active Talk*, Morry Van Ments points out, "Tests have shown that after a ten-minute talk the average listener has heard, understood, properly evaluated and retained only half of what was said, and that half of what is retained will be lost within the next few hours." [4] If that is true, it means that without active listening your child will retain only one-quarter of what the teacher says in class.

Respond. The last ingredient for listening to someone involves responding to what is said. Responding can be a verbal acknowledgment of what the person said, but often it is nonverbal. A nonverbal response can be a nod, a smile, or a forlorn eyebrow that indicates sympathy.

Your child may respond to you without having heard what you said. That is why I put responding after honoring, eye contact, and asking questions. Children (and spouses) are especially skilled at giving a grunt of acknowledgment even though they haven't truly heard you. If that is the case in your home, review all four elements of good listening together.

Practice This Creatively

You can have fun practicing good listening skills. For instance, find a good novel that is recorded on audiocassette. As a family, listen to a few minutes of it each night and discuss it briefly afterward. Not only will you be exercising your listening skills, but you will be hearing someone model good speaking skills as well. After you have listened to a good book on tape, you could make your own audiocassette recording of a favorite short story. Take turns reading aloud into the microphone. When you are done, listen to what you recorded to hear how well each person enunciated the words and dramatized the story.

You could make your own family tape recording to send to a friend or relative. That gives each family member the chance to speak extemporaneously and hear what he or she sounds like. On the tape you can tell funny family stories and give the family news report.

Conversations About Thinking Skills

It will help your child to have conversations that deal directly with a particular thinking skill. This can best be done by using a child's tangible experience, such as an activity or homework. These kinds of conversations should be instructive without being lectures.

Following are a few examples of how conversations might occur in which a particular thinking skill is being practiced. Remember, it will help your child understand how his thinking process works if you tell him the thinking skill he is (or you are) using. As he makes conscious use of a specific thinking skill, he can use the skill again at school on his own. These examples are purposely short and simple, but perhaps they can help you visualize how to use these ideas in your home.

Comparison

Comparison is a good technique for finding similarities between two or more things. To do this skill well you must

(1) break each thing into its parts and (2) match similar parts from one thing with the parts from the other thing.

Son: I think I'd like to play Little League baseball this year, but I don't know if I'm good enough.

Mom: You did well at football last year. Let's compare the two sports. Comparison means finding things that are similar between two different things. What skills did you use for football that will be good for baseball?

Son: Well, I had to be a fast runner. You need that for baseball.

Mom: You are fast. What else?

Son: I don't know.

Mom: Let's make a list that compares baseball with football.

Contrast

Contrasting two or more things often helps you better see their uniqueness. It is sometimes helpful to get a better understanding of something by seeing what it is not. Contrasting simply means focusing on what is different about things.

Daughter: I'm supposed to write a report on the Eiffel Tower, but I don't know where to start.

Dad: Sometimes it helps to start by contrasting one thing with another thing. Contrasting means you highlight the differences between two or more things. For instance, let's look in the encyclopedia and list five ways the Eiffel Tower is different from the Empire State Building.

(After reading)

Daughter: The Eiffel Tower isn't an office building. It is 984 feet tall, and the Empire State Building is 1,250 feet tall. The Eiffel Tower was built in the 1800s and the Empire State Building was built in the 1900s. It is made of iron while the Empire State Building is made of steel and concrete. One is in Europe and the other one is in America.

Dad: Good. Now, you have a better idea of how unique the Eiffel Tower is. Keep that in mind as you write your report. In fact, you can use a few of these contrasts as you write.

Synthesis

Synthesis means bringing different things together to create a new thing. The elements of the different things blend together in a new way. The skill of synthesis is important in creative problem solving. It requires you to (1) define the problem or goal, (2) break each item or piece of information into its parts, (3) mentally put the individual parts together in new combinations, and (4) judge whether the new combination solves your problem or meets your goal.

Son: I'm supposed to write a creative paper on what I would do to solve the traffic congestion in our city. I don't know what to say.

Dad: Synthesis might help you out.

Son: What's that?

Dad: Synthesis means you put together two or more things to create an entirely new thing. The things don't have to be similar at all. By taking two ideas and blending them, sometimes you can come up with a way to solve your problem. What are some different ideas people have for solving traffic problems?

Son: People can take a subway or a train. People can carpool. People can take buses.

Dad: Let's see if we can blend the ideas together and keep the benefits of each one while creating a new means of transportation.

(They think awhile.)

Son: We could radically increase the number of buses, give them special lanes on the freeways—almost like tracks for a train—increase their routes so they are as convenient as carpooling, and make the seats more comfortable and include cellular phones so they are like a nice car.

Summarization

Summarization is important for understanding and remembering information. If you can summarize something, it generally means you understand it fairly well. It also helps you package the information in convenient categories for memorizing. This skill requires that you (1) choose the most important events from the information, (2) put them in their proper sequence, and (3) retell them in your own words.

Daughter: My teacher wants me to write a one-page summary of the story we've been reading. Can you help me?

Mom: Being able to summarize something is an important thinking skill. Summarization requires that you choose the most important events from the story and put them in their proper sequence. So the question you need to ask yourself is, "What were the major events in the story?"

Daughter: That's easy.

Mom: The thing you need to be careful of is that you stick with the most important parts of the story. Each person's summary of a story may be slightly different because people might have differing opinions as to what the most important parts of a story are.

Daughter: And then I put them in the right order.

Mom: Right.

Analysis

Analysis means to break something into its individual parts in order to better understand the whole. To analyze something you need to ask, (1) What are the individual parts that make up the whole? and (2) How much do I need to break apart the whole in order to study it?

Son: I really liked the spaghetti sauce we had last week for dinner. Can we get that same flavor on our pizza tonight?

Mom: We have to analyze what was in the spaghetti sauce to know what to add to the pizza. Analyzing something means breaking it into its parts. Describe the flavor you liked in the sauce.

Son: It was sweet but not like sugar.

Mom: Here's the recipe I used. Let's analyze each ingredient.

Son: It wasn't the tomato paste. It wasn't the hamburger. It couldn't have been the garlic. I don't know what parsley, oregano, bay leaf, or tarragon taste like.

Mom: Go to the spice cabinet and smell each one to see if one is what you liked.

Son: Here it is! It's tarragon.

Mom: Good analysis!

Fact Versus Opinion

When reading or listening to information, it is important to be able to discern fact from opinion. A fact is something you can verify in person or through a reliable source. It is objectively real. An opinion is a value judgment about something. The skill of discernment requires that you ask, (1) Can this be verified objectively? and, (2) Is this someone's value judgment?

Daughter: The newspaper editorial says that the ten people at last night's school board meeting who spoke out against the proposed swimming pool at school didn't make any sense with their reasons. Why can't people be more logical about stuff like this?

Dad: You can't simply believe the newspaper writer when he writes that the people's arguments didn't make any sense. It is important when you read to discern between facts and opinions.

Daughter: Isn't it a fact that the people didn't make any sense?

Dad: No. Facts are things you can verify as true. Opinions are personal value judgments about things. It is the writer's personal judgment that the arguments didn't make sense. To be an objective reader, you have to withhold your judgment until you know the facts, which in this case would be what the ten people actually said. Once you know what they said, then you can have an opinion on whether it made sense. Now, what are the facts in this case?

Daughter: Ten people spoke against the proposed swimming pool. The school board meeting took place last night. The board voted to delay a final decision for one more month.

Dad: And what are the value judgments the writer expressed?

Daughter: That the delayed decision was not necessary and that the people objecting to the pool did not have good reasons for being against it.

Classify

Classifying information means grouping together things that have something in common and then labeling the group. We see many everyday examples of classifications, such as the way food is classified in grocery stores or the way news is classified in the newspaper. Classifying requires the skills of (1) understanding the goal or common features you want to see, (2) skimming the information and taking note of its features, (3) finding other pieces of information that share something in common and putting them together, and (4) creating a label to attach to the group.

Dad: I need you to help me clean the garage today. I want to categorize and store everything in there, and I need your help. It will be a good way to practice the thinking skill of classification.

Son: What is classification?

Dad: It means grouping things together based on their common features. The first step in classifying anything is knowing what your goal is. Our goal is to divide our shelves into areas of things related to the car, the yard, tools, recreation, and furniture storage. Next, as you look at each item, ask yourself into which category each thing fits best.

Son: Here's the car wax buffer. It's for the car, but it's also a tool. Which classification should we give it?

Dad: Good question. Compare it to the other tools. Would it fit better with a hammer, a saw, or a screwdriver?

Son: It's a tool that we use only on the car. The hammer, saw, and screwdriver can be used on many things. I'd say it fits better to classify it with the car.

Dad: That's a great choice! You understand how to classify things.

Son: We don't have a classification for all these cans of paint. It's for the house, but it isn't for furniture or the yard. Let's make a new classification and label it "Paint."

Relevance

Knowing how to determine the relevance of something is an important thinking skill for your child. It will help him weed out important information from trivia. It will help him stick with the main idea when listening to the teacher or reading the textbook. The steps to determining relevance are: (1) have a clear idea of the topic, (2) decide what makes something pertinent to the topic, (3) break the material into pieces (analysis), and measure each piece against your standard of pertinence, and (4) judge how much each piece matches your standard to determine its degree of relevance. Once your child becomes proficient at this process, she can do it with ease while taking notes in class or reading a book.

Daughter: I have to write a paper on the pioneers, but there are so many books in the library I don't know where to start.

Mom: There is an important thinking skill that can help you here. It's called finding relevance.

Daughter: What do you mean?

Mom: Part of your problem is that the subject is too broad. What is a specific topic about the pioneers that you would like to write about?

Daughter: I thought it would be neat to do a paper on what they wore.

Mom: That's great! Now, to find relevant topics, list some things that relate to what they wore as pioneers.

Daughter: Well, anything related to fashion.

Mom: Now, look in the index of several books under the subject of fashion or dress and see if you can find anything. Make notes on anything that matches "pioneers" and the way they dressed. As you read, ask yourself, "Does this relate to my topic?"

These examples are of tangible experiences rather than abstract ideas. Studies have found that conversations at home generally center around things that are familiar, with experiences and tasks that are tangible and immediately applicable. At school, however, discussions often center around abstract ideas that are not imbedded in a direct experience. It would follow, then, that to be successful in school it is important that your child be exposed to conversations on concepts and ideas at home. Whenever you can, try to engage your child in conversations about abstract ideas such as politics, theology, ethics, historical events, or artistic values. That will give your child the chance to exercise his thinking skills.

Conversation About School

Having conversations about your child's schoolwork and experience is very important. Allowing time for your child to tell you what happened each day will give you insight into how well he is doing and what his interests are.

Every parent has experienced the dead-end conversation when it comes to schoolwork. Dead-end conversations happen when you ask, "What did you do in school today?" and your child answers, "Nothing." To avoid such dead ends, narrow the focus of the question. Here is a list of questions that will open up those closed conversations:

What teacher do you like the least (most) and why?

What homework do you have in math tonight?

If you could be the teacher, what would you change about school?

Tell me the best and worst thing that happened to you in school today.

Show me the notes you took in class today. (Discuss them.)

Explain one thing you learned today.

Who was the first person you talked to at school today? What did you say?

What was the most frustrating thing you did today?

In what class did you have the most fun today? Why?

What is one goal you accomplished today at school?

Discussing Problems

If your child is experiencing a problem at school, you need to determine exactly what the problem is, what needs to be done (and by whom) to solve the problem, and how you can tell if the problem has been solved. It is important when you probe for problems that your child not sense that you are criticizing him. It may help to explain that a problem is separate from the person. Think of the problem as a separate entity—a third party.

If your child opens up to you and tells you of a struggle he is having, he is taking a risk. He risks being ridiculed or criticized. Diffuse any anxiety he may have about admitting a weakness by accepting him while at the same time focusing on the problem. It is a good idea to gauge your response according to your child's attitude to the problem. If he is struggling in math class but shows little concern, you should increase your level of concern. If, on the other hand, he is in despair over his math struggles, show less concern and more confidence in his ability to overcome the problem.

Gently probe for the problem. It may not be readily apparent. The cause could range from his not understanding the academic procedure to being distracted by a classmate. Ask questions to get to the root cause.

Johnny: I hate my history class! The teacher doesn't care if we learn anything at all. She moves too fast.

Parent: It sounds frustrating. What are you studying right now?

Johnny: The three branches of government.

Parent: How long has she spent on that?

Johnny: All week.

Parent: Let me see your notes from class.

Johnny: I don't have any. I never know what to write down.

(The real problem may be his lack of note-taking skills.)

Once you have identified the real problem, you need to devise a plan to solve it together. That may be as simple as asking the teacher to move your child closer to the chalkboard or teaching your child a specific step in the academic subject. Determining a solution together will help your child take ownership of the learning goal. It will also teach him that he can overcome obstacles and setbacks. Finally, you need to have a way to monitor his progress. In the example above, the parent simply needs to check with Johnny the next day to see if he took careful notes.

Summary

Conversations with your child help her develop thinking skills. Not only is it important to have a variety of conversations with her, but it is also helpful to explain how good conversations work and what type of thinking goes into elaborate conversations. Well-rounded conversations involve four ingredients: telling about experiences, making comments, asking questions, and listening. You can teach these parts to your child and give her many opportunities for practice. You can also talk with her about various thinking skills and use conversations about everyday activities to teach her how to sharpen her thinking. In the next chapter we will look at how to help your child think about spiritual things.

10
Dig Deeper

Parent Power Tool #8: Emphasize Spiritual Growth

Your Goal
We not only attend church on a regular basis, but I actively set spiritual growth goals for my children's development and seek ways to accomplish those spiritual milestones. I am helping them grow in their understanding of who God is, what He promises us, and how we can walk with Him.

Your child can do tremendously well in school and still not be satisfied with life or be a positive influence in the lives of others. If the knowledge in your child's head is not guided by wisdom in his heart, he can easily steer the ship of his life into the rocks of despair. In this chapter we will focus on how you can help your child live the examined life—a life that recognizes its spiritual hunger and seeks to fill it with meaning and purpose. At some point, if it hasn't happened already, your child will face challenges to his faith from others. Friends may ask him why he attends church or why he believes the way he does. Certainly he will be challenged to defend himself against the lure of ideas from popular culture.

You can guide him through these challenges by helping him understand the importance of seeking answers to spiritual questions. This chapter offers you one way to help your child understand God.

The Need

It seems that like no other era before us, we live in a time in need of great spiritual renewal. Our souls are easily perverted by our society's emphasis on materialism over meaning and style over substance. A team of professors led by Quentin Schultze observe in the book *Dancing in the Dark* that to get a sense of a society's cultural pulse you can look at the public places around which most people organize their lives. Medieval Europeans organized their lives around the local cathedral. Today, two of the most powerful focal points for many young people are the shopping mall and the television set.[1]

On weekends they congregate at the mall, and each night they gather and passively receive our culture through television. Few young people contribute to the dynamics of our culture because they are too busy having it fed to them electronically. Schultze comments, "Adolescents often care far more about the content and style of media made thousands of miles away than about what takes place in their own neighborhoods and even in their own families."[2] And important spiritual questions—What is important? Who am I? What do I want out of life?—are answered at these gatherings: "Buy this to be happy!" "Seek quick gratification!" "Live for the moment!" "There is no truth, only opinions on talk shows."

Not only does television shape your child's thinking, but music is another powerful influence. One MTV executive explained to the *Philadelphia Inquirer*, "Music tends to be a predictor of behavior and social values. You tell me the music people like and I'll tell you their views on abortion, whether we should increase our military arms, and what their sense of humor is like."[3]

Is all popular music bad? Certainly not. Will listening to rock music automatically corrupt your child? Not likely. Having fun, creating a mood, being caught up in a song is not evil. But what messages is your teenager receiving from his music? What attitudes does it create? And where is it directing his time and attention? Popular music engulfs a young person like radiation invades the body. Radiation can help (as in an x-ray) or harm (as in a nuclear bomb). But even when it is used for good purposes, the x-ray technician must stand behind a lead-lined protection to guard against overexposure.

Part of humans' spiritual quest has always been to define "the good life." The electronically fed pop culture creates the illusion of fulfilling this quest through its own definition of the good life. What it actually delivers to young people, however, is a saccharine diet—momentarily sweet but devoid of sustenance.

Pop Culture and School

When it comes to the search for truth, unfortunately, the electronic media and public education have become ideological bedfellows in promoting one spiritually devastating theme: Real truth is an illusion, each person must find his or her own way. This is called *relativism*. In *The Closing of the American Mind*, Professor Allan Bloom laments that so many high school students graduate believing in relativism—that is, that there is no right or wrong:

> There is one thing a professor can be absolutely certain of: almost every student entering the university believes, or says he believes, that truth is relative. . . . They have all been equipped with this framework early on, and it is the modern replacement for the inalienable natural rights that used to be the traditional American grounds for a free society. . . . The danger they have been taught to fear from absolutism is not error but intolerance. Relativism is necessary to openness; and this is the virtue, the only virtue, which all primary education for more than fifty years has dedicated itself to inculcating. . . . Openness . . . is the great insight of our times.[4]

The problem created by this "openness" is that young people grow up alone and adrift in a sea of uncertainty. They have cut themselves loose (or have been cut loose) from the chains of tradition, yet they don't know where they are headed. They are ships without rudders on windy seas with no sails. What is worse, they believe they need no rudder.

This shift in education from a quest for life's meaning to being a socializer through relativism is largely due to the lack of consensus among education planners regarding what is ultimately meaningful in life. Your child won't get a strong direction regarding life's meaning in the classroom. In order for your child to form a meaningful worldview, you must help him. A spiritual orientation is the garden hose through which the water of education flows. It determines where the refreshment of education will be directed—on the flower bed of life or wasted in the gutter. That is why it is so important for you to carefully consider the spiritual perspective you are giving your child.

Helping Your Teenager

Your older children will encounter some form of relativism in the music they hear, the movies they see, and possibly in some things they are taught at school. Once they are old enough, they can understand when you teach them about relativism.

You can point out that the problem of relativism is that it makes no sense. To say that *all* things are relative and that there are no absolutes is, in itself, an absolute statement. The one absolute "truth" for the relativist is that all things are relative. If all things are relative, then so is that statement. It, then, is not true. The best that a relativist can say is that some things are relative and some things are absolute. Once he admits that some things are absolute he must determine what those things are.

What You Can Do

1. As you watch television together, point out for your teenager examples of characters who create their own morality. For your younger children, you can make the point that what the TV character is doing or saying is wrong and affirm that what God's Word says is right.
2. Regularly discuss with your children how the Bible defines "the good life."
3. Be a good role model of someone who lives by his or her principles. Let your children see how you make your decisions so they can learn the process of living by convictions.

4. Regularly talk with your children about the spiritual challenges they face at school. That may involve values they are taught, challenges to their faith from their peers, or temptations to do the wrong thing at school. Every discussion does not have to end with a lecture on what is right. Make yourself available as an understanding guide for your child.

Your child's greatest need is for a spiritual foundation upon which he can build the rest of his education. Without such a foundation his life is an empty pursuit of passing fancies. As humans we have a deep longing for meaning and purpose. A spiritual foundation provides this. In the rest of this chapter, I suggest a framework for developing your family's spiritual "curriculum." I use the imagery of being a child of the King and living in His palace.

Living in the Palace of the King

A remarkable thing occurs when we become Christians. God makes us spiritually alive. In the physical world we do not look any different than we did before we came to God through Jesus Christ, but inside a new creature is born. We are alive to God and to His Spirit working in us. This incredible phenomenon happens to us whether we are sixty years old or six years old. If your children have come to know salvation through Christ, they are altogether different from other human beings. They are not only human, but they are spiritually alive humans—a new species. This gives them access to tremendous spiritual tools provided by God for us while we are here on earth. Being both physically and spiritually alive, they must use divine apparatus to function properly in the world. God's main concern is for your children's spiritual well-being. He is concerned about what will draw your children to a closer relationship with Him. The physical and emotional benefits of this relationship, though secondary to the spiritual benefits, are very real.

Using God's spiritual resources, your children can experience contentment in life and not succumb to the consumerism they see on television; they can have composure and self-assurance in the midst of pressure situations at school; they can express compassion and kindness toward those around them; they can make good decisions and show discernment in all areas of their lives; they can exercise control over their emotions and impulses; and they can express a positive attitude toward their futures and the lives of others. They can be bulletproofed from harm, in a sense, while they move through school and on to adulthood. They can build a kind of spiritual self-confidence, confident in their ability to tap the spiritual resources God has graciously provided for each believer—young or old.

You should focus on developing three spiritual resources in your children. The three tools center around a hope in biblical truths: what the Bible tells us God will do for us, what it tells us God is like, and what it tells us about how God operates. Hope is a confident assurance that what God says, He will do; that the way He describes Himself is accurate; and that the principles by which He operates are consistent. To the degree that your children have a confident assurance—a hope—in biblical truths, they can have a spiritually empowered confidence in life.

Confidence in Our Royal Position

Every Christian has been adopted into the royal family of God. This status brings many spiritual privileges and assets as well as royal protocol. As the Scriptures tell us, we are blessed "with every spiritual blessing in the heavenly places in Christ" (Eph. 1:3), and we are to please God by operating "according to the rules" (2 Tim. 2:5). When we come to God through salvation, we are not only placed in God's kingdom, but in His palace as well. In Psalm 23:6, David talks of dwelling "in the house of the LORD forever." Just as God's kingdom is spiritual, so His palace is spiritual. This magnificently furnished spiritual structure is the place of refreshment, relaxation, and protection as we go through life. We can enjoy spiritual refreshment that radiates into our day-to-day life. David refers to this in

Psalm 16:11 when he writes, "In Thy presence is fulness of joy; in Thy right hand are pleasures forever." That symbolizes our fellowship with the King. In His presence at the palace are tremendous spiritual resources for dealing with the trials of life. We are to come to the "throne of grace, that we may receive mercy and may find grace to help in time of need" (Heb. 4:16).

How do we enjoy those eternal pleasures? How do we experience that sense of joy in His presence? Your children need to understand the tremendous tools the King has given them to move through this life with confidence, making healthy decisions, and growing in favor before God and man.

Does growing in the Christian life simply mean going to church week after week, hoping that something will sink into our children's minds and change their hearts; or is there a definite plan we can follow in nurturing children and young people to spiritual maturity, even at a young age? I believe there is a plan you can follow and milestones you can strive for in the growth of your children. The Scriptures are full of examples of young men and women who expressed mature attitudes toward the Lord (see 2 Tim. 3:15). Each biblical character, whether it was young David, Daniel, Joseph, Esther, Mary, or Timothy, expressed hope in the three categories of biblical truth. These categories make up the pattern by which you can plan a spiritual growth curriculum for your children. These resources can be pictured as existing in rooms within God's palace of fellowship.

The three resources in which we place our hope are:

A. Portraits of God
B. Promises of God
C. Protocols of God

God's Hall of Portraits

Imagine the massive palace of God with His throne at its center. This palace is your spiritual home—it is where you dwell. Picture yourself walking down a great hall that leads to the throne room of God. The hall is full of painted portraits. These are no ordinary masterpieces. Each one shows a piece of the Master. Each one portrays God in a different light and in a different stance. In one, He is shown as a judge. In another, a loving friend. In another, He is standing firm as an unchanging rock.

The portraits of God throughout the Bible help us understand in whom we place our faith and hope. In theological terms, these are God's attributes. But it may be easier to think of them in terms of word pictures that describe God. These portraits of God help to deepen our admiration and awe for Him. This is the essence of a personal love for God. As we begin to understand more about the King, we grow in our appreciation for Him. Not only does that increase our devotion to Him, it also gives us another important resource to draw from.

At times we can draw greater strength by placing our hope in God's love. At other times we can be sustained more easily by focusing on His justice. We may need to concentrate our hope in His almighty power or His grace or His mercy. Having a richer understanding of the King means we can both draw upon His strength in time of need and increase our love for Him throughout our lives. Our admiration and awe for Him leads to a life of devotion to and love for Him. These are some of the biblical portraits of God you can introduce your children to:

Holy . . . . Isaiah 6:3; Revelation 15:4; 1 Peter 1:15,16

Just . . . . Psalm 19:9,10; Isaiah 33:22; 1 Peter 1:17

Righteous . . . . . : . . . Psalm 11:7; Psalm 50:6; 1 John 3:7

Eternal . . . . Psalm 45:6; Psalm 90:1,2; 1 Timothy 1:17

Unchanging . . . . Malachi 3:6; James 1:17

Wise . . . . Daniel 2:20; Psalm 147:5; James 1:5

All-Powerful . . . . . . Psalm 62:11; Revelation 19:6
(Omnipotent)

All-Knowing . . . . . . Psalm 44:21; Psalm 139:4; Hebrews 4:13
(Omniscient)

Ever-Present . . . . . . Psalm 139:7–10; Jeremiah 23:24
(Omnipresent)

Good . . . . Psalm 52:1; Psalm 145:9; Nahum 1:7
Merciful . . . . 1 Chronicles 16:34; Psalm 62:12; Psalm 138:8
Gracious . . . . Jonah 4:2; Romans 3:24; Titus 2:11
Loving. . . . . Jeremiah 31:3; Romans 8:39; 1 John 4:16
Sovereign . . . . Psalm 97:1; Proverbs 21:1; Jude 1:25
Triune. . . . . Colossians 2:9; 1 John 5:7
Infinite . . . . Psalm 147:5; 1 Kings 8:27

It would be beneficial for you and your child to study each portrait of God. As you examine each portrait, ask three questions:

1. What does the portrait look like? (Study the characteristic.)
2. How does the portrait affect my life?
3. What should be my response to God and to others because of this portrait?

You might start by examining God's holiness. In your study, you can spend some time reading Scripture that reveals His purity. Then ask the question, "How does this attribute of God impact my life?" and, "What should be my response to this characteristic?" As we gain a better idea, for instance, of His holiness, we are humbled in our view of ourselves. This not only affects how we approach God but also how we interact with people. This humble perspective helps us treat others with respect. It prompts us to be inclusive of people rather than form cliques and project a better-than-thou attitude. It helps us empathize with the suffering of others because we are no better than they are. We realize just how unholy and unworthy we are compared to God. It doesn't matter how beautiful or talented we are. In the eyes of God, we are all equally sinners.

By teaching your child about God's portraits and discussing ways each one applies to our lives, you are showing your child that an understanding of God's person has practical application. One way to apply each portrait is to look for the promises that are attached to each one.

The Treasure Room of God's Promises

At the end of the Hall of Portraits is the throne of God. Picture a large room that opens to the right of the throne of God. When we look inside, we see an endless hall filled with sparkling treasures. The promises of God are tremendous treasures that we can dip into from the King's palace and use any time we want, and we can take as much as we want. In fact, God sits on His throne and exhorts us to take more of His treasures than we often are willing to take. Each time we open the door of His treasure house to look at His marvelous riches, He bids us to fill our arms with His gold. I find in my own life that most often my response is to pick up only one coin and put it in my pocket. "This," I say to myself, "is a real blessing." Yet I often lack the desire to accept the armload of treasure He so lovingly urges upon me.

As an adopted child of the King, I have full access to hundreds of specific promises that I can draw upon for strength in time of need. God wants me to enjoy His grace more than I want to enjoy it. He wants me to revel in His forgiveness more than I want to. He wants me to draw upon the promises of His power, guidance, and protection more than I care to even explore.

Tapping into His storehouse does more than simply psyche us up to cope with a trial. A spiritual fusion happens when we use our hope in the promises of God. God's Spirit ministers to our spirit (see 1 Cor. 2:12–14). The Christian life is a supernatural life lived in a supernatural way.

Christianity isn't just about having a positive mental attitude. It means we direct our hope toward God's promises. When we do this, God's Spirit actually begins to pour blessings into our attitudes, emotions, and actions. These blessings are outside our natural experience. They are supernatural. But they are triggered by our hope in God.

This is not to say we earn God's blessings. We simply recognize spiritual realities and place our trust in those realities. There is no merit before God for that recognition, any more than there is merit for recognizing the reality of gravity.

However, just as we can benefit from using our knowledge of gravity by jumping up in the air with the assurance we will land back on the ground, we can benefit from relying on the promises of God.

We access God's promises, as we do all biblical truths, through our memories combined with our ability to trust. It is vitally important, therefore, that we know the promises of God. Here are just a few of His promises in which your child can place his hope:

Physical endurance through natural disaster (Psalm 46:1–3)
Emotional endurance through hardships (Psalm 27:14)
Freedom from anxiety (Phil. 4:6–7)
Blessings for having proper priorities (Psalm 1:1–3)
Courage in the face of fear (Psalm 31:24)
Eternal life after death (John 3:16)
Blessing in the face of put-downs (Heb. 13:6)
Grace and mercy in time of need (Heb. 4:16)

As a family, you can memorize the promises of God. To help your child establish a verse in her mind after memorizing it, have her use it in a variety of ways: write a note to a grandparent and quote the verse; write in her diary what the verse means or how she can use it; draw a picture representing the concepts in the verse; watch for examples throughout the week where the verse can be applied. One family I know makes up a song using the verse. They have fun singing it to each other throughout the week and find that it helps them remember the words.

The Protocol of God

Picture a great room to the left of God's throne. There is the hall of protocol. It is lined with mirrors from floor to ceiling. In the center of the hall and running its entire length are tables of scrolls. On the scrolls are the protocol principles of God. As adopted children in the royal family of God, we must conform to the royal protocol—the precisely correct way of doing things. In God's plan, the right thing done in the wrong way is wrong. The end does not justify the means. This royal protocol comes from God's character. We are in His presence at the royal court at all times; thus, we must live according to His royal protocol at all times.

Once we read and learn the divine protocol, we look at ourselves in the mirror. The question we must ask is, "Am I living by the royal protocol?" James 1:23–25 uses the analogy of the mirror to instruct us in self-examination by the light of God's protocol:

> For if anyone is a hearer of the word [protocol principle] and not a doer, he is like a man who looks at his natural face in a mirror; for once he has looked at himself [using the standards of divine protocol] and gone away, he has immediately forgotten what kind of person he was [non-conformity to protocol]. But one who looks intently at the perfect law [protocol plan of God], the law of liberty, and abides by it, not having become a forgetful hearer [saturation of his soul with biblical principles] but an effectual doer [conformity to protocol], this man shall be blessed in what he does.

God's Word is a mirror that helps us see who we really are and how we are living.

Your children have been adopted into the royal family of God. They live in the palace of the Most High. They play and study and sleep before the throne of the Almighty (Matt. 18:10). Such royal status demands royal protocol. We tend to think of the protocol of God as being about moral living. His protocol includes morality but goes far beyond it.

The principles of God have to do with the way God operates and the way He expects believers to operate. The Bible has many protocol instructions, and I have listed just a few.

- God responds to those who are humble (James 4:6).
- We must regularly confess our sins to God (1 John 1:9).

- God leads those who trust Him (Prov. 3:5–6).
- Anxiety is stopped through hope in God (Phil.4:6–7).
- Work as unto the Lord, not for men (Eph. 6:7).

Those instructions represent the ways God wants us to function as Christians. For instance, we are to do our best in our work because we are doing it to please God, not men. That means we have internal motivation for producing quality work. A proper understanding about work means that God is our quality-control manager. Such a perspective will help your teenager develop a strong work ethic. It is not enough to just perform at our minimal effort. God's protocol for work is to diligently give our best effort.

As you have family devotions and discuss God's protocol, talk about real-world applications of a specific principle. Discuss a problem someone in the family is having. When appropriate, it's a good idea to talk about a difficulty you are going through and let your children see how you apply a protocol principle

Spiritual Confidence

When we focus attention on the promises, portraits, and principles of God, we increase our spiritual confidence. This is not pride. It is a confident recognition that we are responsible for our thoughts, attitudes, and actions. It is the realization that we can direct our thinking toward the promises of God and find hope and confidence for living. We can meditate on a portrait of God and draw strength from His character. We can align with the protocol principles of God and express wisdom and insight beyond what others may expect for our age. We are confident, not in ourselves for strength and answers to life but in our access to the strength drawn from God's promises, portraits, and principles.

In this state of spiritual confidence, the negative effects of peer pressure are reduced. Our concern is not for what others think of us but for what God thinks of us. Likewise, relationships with family, friends, and teachers are enriched. We are not annoyed by others because we respond to them in a love based upon our internal virtue rather than their personal loveliness (or lack of it).

We can truly express love for all people because that love is based upon our internal humility and character. Our personal love for God (admiration and awe directed toward Him) gives us the internal strength of character to express love for others. With spiritual confidence, we eliminate abnormal stress and anxiety. We frequently and consistently access the treasure chest of God's promises; we meander through the hall of His portraits; we study His principles in the great hall of mirrors.

Spiritual confidence can be cultivated in children. However, an important word of caution: avoid training them toward the product instead of the perspective. Spiritual confidence will develop naturally as your children focus on *using* the promises, portraits, and protocols of God. If you exclusively focus on how they "should" be living (product) they can become discouraged and foster feelings of guilt and inadequacy. For example, we *should* be trusting God in all things. However, to encourage this trust, it is better to excite your children about the promises, portraits, and protocol of God than to merely say, "Trust God." To ask someone to trust God without knowing Him is like asking a total stranger to house-sit for you while you are on vacation. If, on the other hand, you asked your best friend to stay in your house while you were away, the issue of trust would never even come up. It would be assumed based upon the intimacy of your relationship.

It is good to have moral expectations for children, but moral expectation without moral explanation creates moral exasperation. Young people—teens especially—do not need moralizing; they need moral-energizing. While maintaining moral expectations, it is wise to help your child see the moral behavior from a larger, divine perspective. We behave certain ways because God's character demands a protocol. His demands are for our good physically and emotionally, as well as spiritually.

This need not be an abstract explanation for your children. Point out examples of people who have violated God's protocol for living and have been hurt physically or emotionally. Help them feel the emotional well-being of following God's protocol. This is how a person develops a divinely oriented perspective. Be careful that this does not degenerate into self-righteous gossip. It is best to use examples in the news or on television, instead of friends and family.

In the Next Thirty Days

In the next thirty days begin a regular program of introducing your children to the full range of the portraits of God. For example, every two weeks choose a different portrait around which to center your family devotions. During that two-week period, read Scripture passages that not only explain an attribute of God in the abstract (such as His goodness) but also show that attribute in action through Bible stories. Then, look for examples of how that portrait of God is revealed in your family's life.

You can weave God's promises into your family devotions as well and even attach a promise of God to each portrait of God. For example, God's goodness is declared in Nahum 1:7. It is demonstrated in Exodus 16 when God provided manna for His people. It can be seen in His provision for your family each day. His goodness is behind His promise to us when Peter tells us to be "casting all your anxiety upon Him, because He cares for you" (1 Pet. 5:7). That passage also reveals a protocol principle of God: We can conquer our worries by placing our faith in God's goodness and our hope in His promise to care for us.

Summary

It is one thing to outline the three resources of God, but it is quite another to consistently use them. Yet that is the maturing process of the Christian life. Every day I must calm my anxious heart or soothe my wounded spirit or temper my self-enthroning plans and remind myself of these three royal assets. Frequently, I must open God's treasure chest to find the right promise in my time of need. It is not always easy and I don't always do it, but each time I lean upon a promise of God, each time I find comfort in His portrait, each time I find success by following His protocol, my confidence is increased. That is what it means for your children to put on the whole armor of God (see Eph. 6).

Teaching these principles to your children can be both formal, in a time of family study and discussion, and informal as you go through your day together. Being together as family provides the opportunity for wonderful learning experiences. The next chapter shows how to maximize family togetherness.

11

Create Togetherness

Parent Power Tool #9: Promote Family Togetherness

Your Goal
We spend more than three hours each week in a fun or stimulating family activity. I make a point of telling family stories and creating family traditions. Our family is an emotionally secure place for my children to grow up.

A family's experience together is like a rope: It can hold you secure like mountain climbers as you scale the challenges of life, or it can be turned into a hangman's noose and strangle the life out of you. I know, as a teacher, the impact a family's home environment can have on a student's learning. I have seen bright students' schoolwork suffer because of trouble at home.

Think back on your own experience as a child. Focus, for a moment, on the amount of time your parents spent with you. Did you go places frequently as a family? Do you remember good times at restaurants, musical productions, plays, vacations, or sports events? Did you spend time together at home without the television set on? How often did you play games together, work on a hobby, eat meals together, or talk about personal matters?

You may recall things your parents did with you that you want to do with your children, and you may remember things that you want to do differently. Your apprenticeship for parenthood—that is, your own childhood—largely shaped the values, expectations, and behaviors you now exhibit as a parent. You watched your father and mother interact as a couple. You learned what was valued in your family and what was not. You saw a thousand things modeled by your parents. And, like it or not, you will most likely repeat many of them yourself. Your parents might have been wonderful role models, or they might have been parental disasters. Either way it will be a good exercise for you to create three lists.

First, take a few minutes and list the ways your family spent time together. On a piece of paper (or on several pieces) write category headings of: vacations, mealtimes, cultural events, family games, sports and recreation, religious services, and personal talk times. Under each category list the actual places you went, games you played, things you did, or talks you remember having.

Create a second list of behaviors, attitudes, and values your parents exhibited that you want to repeat in your family and those things that you don't want to repeat.

Now, take some time to make a list of the things you already do with your kids. Try to be specific.

Finally, the question that cuts to the heart of the matter is this: Are you doing the good things or the bad things your parents did? A little self-awareness here can help you make appropriate adjustments to how you spend time together as a family. Since family times together are like the rope that can either help you or hang you, you might ask yourself whether the times you spend with your children are lifelines or nooses.

The Impact on Learning

Quality and quantity time spent together create a tremendous platform for learning. Your family atmosphere creates spoken and unspoken priorities, goals, attitudes, and ideas about the world. Through your attitudes and actions your family develops assumptions about life. Is life an adventure or a burden? Is it okay to risk failure, or should you play it safe? Does political involvement matter, or is it out of your control? Is education important for personal refinement or just for getting a job? Can intimacy with others be achieved, or should you keep others at arm's length? These are just a few of the assumptions that might be woven into the fabric of your family.

Each member of your family tends to share the most basic assumptions you create. These assumptions affect your child's learning. They affect the way he approaches the discovery of new things. They affect the way he interacts with teachers and peers. They affect the way he views his homework.

As you read this chapter, think about the things you do that shape the way your child approaches life. One important thread in the lifeline of a family is the love and acceptance each member expresses to others.

Love with Skin on It

During a particularly violent thunderstorm, a frightened little girl clung to her daddy's arm. He tried to comfort her by explaining that she didn't need to be afraid since God loved her.

"I know God loves me," she replied. "But right now I want someone with skin on to love me."

Love with skin on is the huggable kind. The first requirement of family togetherness is actually being together. That may seem obvious, but it is getting harder and harder to do. Now that many families have parents who both work outside the home, family togetherness is in serious jeopardy. In the best-selling book *A Passion for Excellence*, the authors make this observation in the chapter "What Price Excellence?":

We have found that the majority of passionate activists who hammer away at the old boundaries have given up family vacations, Little League games, birthday dinners, evenings, weekends and lunch hours, gardening, reading, movies and most other pastimes. We have a number of friends whose marriages or partnerships crumbled under the weight of their devotion to a dream. There are more newly single parents than we expected among our colleagues. . . . We are frequently asked if it is possible to "have it all"—a full and satisfying personal life and a full and satisfying, hard-working, professional one. Our answer is: No. The price of excellence is time, energy, attention and focus, at the very same time that energy, attention, and focus could have gone toward enjoying your daughter's soccer game. . . . But we think the renewed sense of purpose, of making a difference, of recovered self-respect, is well worth the price of admission.[1]

It makes you wonder what is so "excellent" about a life of business success that promotes personal failure. When you are in the hospital with cancer, will your stockholders be by your bedside? Will it be your boss who comforts you when your neglected teenager commits suicide? At the end of your life, will you wish you spent more time at the office or with your children? Does excellence taste so delicious that you'd rather enjoy it alone—having sacrificed your marriage along the way—rather than settle for something less "excellent" that tastes all the more sweet because it is being shared by two?

Moving Your Fences

Family togetherness is more than simply spending time with each other, however. It means family cohesiveness, family supportiveness, and family oneness. Your family should be the one safe place where your child can fail in an endeavor. Personal growth requires a certain amount of risk taking. Your children need the courage to try something new, to venture into a new sport, hobby, or academic subject. They need to do that in an environment in which it is safe to fail, a place where there is no risk of ridicule.

Look up the word *acceptance* in the dictionary and you will find that it is described as approval, belief in something, or receiving something. The picture is of open arms and affirming words. Though you may not always approve of your child's behaviors, acceptance means you always approve of his person.

There is a tender story that illustrates acceptance. During World War II, some French soldiers brought the body of a dead comrade to a cemetery on the property of a church. The priest inquired of the soldiers whether their deceased comrade had been a baptized member of the Roman Catholic Church. They said they did not know. The priest informed them that, in that case, the soldier could not be buried on church property. The soldiers took the body and gave it the most dignified burial they could just outside the churchyard fence. The next day as they were leaving the small town they passed by the church and decided to pay their respects to their comrade one last time. To their astonishment they could not find his grave site. As they were leaving in bewilderment the priest walked up. He told them that during the night he felt so bad about excluding his fallen countryman that he awoke early and, with his own hands, uprooted the fence and moved it to include the body of the soldier who had sacrificed his life for France.

Accepting one another requires that we move the fences of our defenses to include the frailties of our family. We all have territory that we defend. We vainly attempt to defend our intellect when we say to another, "I told you so." We attempt to defend our moral superiority over others when we condemn with, "I would never do that." So many words that are meant to build fences to keep our children in the family territory only end up keeping them out. Words we intend to use for discipline come out as ridicule—"Why are you so stupid?!" Words we use to protect our children end up harming them—"You can't seem to do anything right, can you?!" If the first requirement of family togetherness is to be together physically, the second is, through acceptance, to be together emotionally. How you treat your children, your spouse, and your friends provides a powerful model for your children to follow.

Role Modeling

A French proverb states that children need models more than they need critics. That could not be more fitting for families today. Who are your child's role models: Madonna? Sylvester Stallone? Metallica? All around her the forces of popular culture model attitudes and behaviors for her to copy.

To a large extent these forces cannot be kept from your child. Popular culture is pervasive. We swim in it. If we turn off the television set, we get it from radio or magazines or school or peers or church. Film critic Michael Medved made this point while delivering a speech to schoolteachers. He asked for a show of hands from the audience of anyone who owned a Madonna album, cassette, or CD. No one did. He then asked if anyone had attended a Madonna concert. No one had. He asked if anyone had read a book about Madonna. Again, no one had. Finally, he asked how many people knew about Madonna? Everyone in the audience raised his hand. You can't escape culture, but you can counter it with your own modeling.

The cultural saturation of questionable role models makes the parents' job as a good role model all the more important. The time you spend together as a family affords you many opportunities for role modeling. Consider just a few of the many roles you model for your child: spouse, parent, taxpayer, church member, worker, neighbor, conversationalist, student, hobbyist, homeowner or renter, driver, passenger, and friend.

Better authors than I have written about how to be a good father or mother, husband or wife. There *is* one insight I can contribute that sounds simple, but I have found it profitable: Good families are made up of good people. You can't have family togetherness when the individuals in the family don't have their own personalities put together well. The focus of your attention should not be on how you *appear* to your child so much as how you *are* as a person. The modeling will follow naturally. Go back to the two lists you created at the beginning of this chapter, and think about the attitudes and behaviors you are modeling for your child. List one or two things you would like to improve in how you model an attitude or behavior for your child.

Below I have listed a few questions you can ask yourself regarding modeling. These questions focus on things you do that could help your child learn. Note that the focus is on what you do, and not what you say.

Do you demonstrate that reading is a priority?
Do you demonstrate respect for teachers?
Do you demonstrate that rebounding from failure can
    lead to success?
Do you demonstrate a strong work ethic?
Do you demonstrate stick-to-it-iveness?
Do you demonstrate problem solving?

Do you demonstrate good television viewing habits?
Do you demonstrate that a particular subject is important
   to learn?

Family Folklore

Every family has its stories. Folklore is the traditional
beliefs, practices, legends, and tales of a people, transmitted
orally. It also includes photographs, films, videotapes, and
family memorabilia. Your family togetherness includes the
creation and transmission of the family folklore. Folklore gives
a family a sense of identity and uniqueness.[2]

Family togetherness includes the telling and retelling of the
family stories. In my family, this included (and still includes)
stories of my father's adventures as a B-17 pilot during World
War II. He told us how, during the end of the war, he landed at
a Nazi airfield occupied by the Russians. He was suspected by
the Russians of being a Nazi trying to escape Berlin and was
thrown in jail overnight until the confusion was cleared up. He
told us of being on the Air Force's ski jumping team in the
Swiss Alps and how he built a small plane during the war from
scrap airplane parts.

From my mother's side of the family, we learned that my
great-grandfather's hair turned white in one day as he was
chased by Indians while pioneering in his covered wagon. We
learned how the family moved west from Missouri during the
Depression to start a new life and how they heated water on
the roof of their small home in order to reduce their electric
bill.

My parents told and retold us how they met and how they
courted and what their first years of marriage were like.
Through this oral history, we learned we were a family of
adventurers. Our parents didn't teach us that overtly, but it
came to us through the family folklore. The accumulation and
unique shaping of your family stories provide a sense of identity for your children. This adds to their sense of well-being,
which is necessary for learning.

Family Traditions

Remember how your family celebrated Christmas or Thanksgiving? Remember when your sister or brother got married or your nephew's first birthday? Family traditions involve rituals, celebrations, and rites of passage. They play a central role in family togetherness and are often the setting for the making of new family stories and photographs capturing the event.

In our family certain traditions were celebrated, for the most part, as cherished rituals. That is, they had definite, even if unspoken, guidelines; they had an element of rigidity and created a sense that "this is the right way of doing it." Just before Christmas, we always went to the same restaurant as a family and drove through a particularly pretty neighborhood to view Christmas lights. Our tree was always decorated with the same "look." One person was designated as the gift distributor, and everyone watched as we took turns opening gifts. Dr. Carlfred Broderick, in his book *Understanding the Family Process*, points out that rituals have the effect of "educating the participants in the values they share, of regulating their behavior, and of celebrating their common identity."[3]

Family traditions can be simple too. You can create them as you pray before each meal, attend religious services weekly, wash the family car on Saturdays, or make an annual back-to-school shopping trip. You can find them in dozens of different actions you perform as a family. They provide a solid riverbed for your family under the swift-moving current of societal change.

You may find it helpful to create a list of some of your current family traditions or create a list of new ones. Consider patterns that you have developed or need to develop surrounding:

- how you begin a meal (with a prayer?)
- how you end your evening (with reading, a prayer?)
- Christmas
- Easter
- Thanksgiving

- summer activities
- family chores
- Saturday mornings
- church activities
- birthdays, anniversaries, and special awards
- recognition of good grades in school

Family togetherness means being together physically and emotionally and, in the process, creating a body of family folklore. When taken together, these things provide a foundation for greater stability for your child that will help him in school. This togetherness also provides for your child a set of values about the world and a ranking of life's priorities. It gives him a frame of reference from which to evaluate and participate in school activities.

Creating Family Togetherness for Learning

Following are some ideas of things you can do to create togetherness both physically and emotionally as well as perpetuate and create family folklore. As you read each idea, think about how you can implement it. Where can you go locally to do it? What materials do you have or do you need to do it? Jot a note in the margin as you think of how you are going to create family togetherness.

The Arts

1. Go to an art museum. Sound boring? That doesn't have to be true. Try to get someone from the museum to give you a narrated tour. Stories about the artists will make their paintings come alive. If there is no tour guide, the information desk may have a brochure on the artists. You can also have fun by creating a challenge for your children. Put together a scavenger hunt. Questions could include: Which painting uses the most red paint (or blue, or green)? Which painting has the most people in it (or animals,

or houses)? Which painting is the happiest, and which is the saddest? Which is the brightest, and which is the darkest? For older children, you might want to have more sophisticated questions about style or the meaning of a painting. Each child can choose the painting he or she likes best and buy a postcard of it in the museum gift shop as a memento.

2. Go to an art gallery. This is similar to going to an art museum, and you are guaranteed to have a salesman to tell you about the paintings. Let him or her know that you are not in the market to buy but want your children to learn about the arts. If he has the time, he will most likely oblige your request for a narration. Often the gallery will have a postcard advertising a particular artist, and they will give you one to take home.

3. Attend a play, an opera, or a ballet. If you can't afford a regular performance, you can often buy lower-priced tickets to the dress rehearsal. The local college, church, or community center may also have inexpensive performances.

4. Create a "museum" at home of your own family's art, complete with a little card next to each piece giving its title, name of artist, and brief explanation of the piece.

5. Write a family play. Have your children dictate the dialogue of a story to you. Create parts for each family member and put on a production. Videotape it and make it a part of your preserved memories.

6. Have a family sing-along. Write a song together or make up new words to a familiar song.

7. Attend a free concert in the park offered through your community. Talk about what kind of music will be played. Where did it come from? Why is it special?

History and Your Community

1. Visit a history museum. Tell your children before you enter that while they are viewing the exhibits,

you want each of them to choose a favorite one and to explain why it is their favorite.

2. Be amateur historians. As a family, create a scrapbook telling the history of your community. Travel to local historic sites such as old churches, cemeteries, city hall and other public buildings, old hotels, bed and breakfast inns, and old factories. Use photographs, postcards, brochures, maps, and other printed materials in your scrapbook. Write descriptions of the historic sites next to the pictures.

3. Research your family's genealogy, and create a family tree.

4. Go to your local courthouse and watch a trial. Most courtrooms are open to the public. Call your courthouse to get details.

Science and Technology

1. Visit an aquarium or fish hatchery.

2. Go to a rocky shore of the ocean and examine marine life in tide pools, or visit a river or creek and catalog all the wildlife you see.

3. Spend an hour collecting a variety of flowers or leaves. When you are done, lay them on a table and examine their differences.

4. Find out if your area is rich in fossils. If it is, spend an afternoon digging for fossils. Create a display case for any you find.

5. Take a short hike in the wilderness, and discover the many varieties of plants and animals and geological features in your community.

6. Take a tour of a factory.

7. Visit a farm and watch how cows are milked or crops are harvested.

8. Drive into the country on a clear night away from city lights, lay blankets in an open field, and watch the stars. Take along a map of the constellations for reference.

Foods

1. Try an exotic restaurant. If you are on a tight budget, you can go to a nice restaurant for the atmosphere and still keep the bill low by eating dinner at home and only ordering a dessert at the restaurant. It would be best to go after the dinner hour so you won't take up a table during peak customer times.

2. Have the whole family help create a picnic with a theme. For example, for a French picnic pack French bread, a variety of cheeses, and sparkling apple juice. Top it off by wearing berets and playing a tape recording of French music. Your themes could be ethnic (Chinese, Italian, Ethiopian), regional (Western, New England, Southern), or just about anything your imagination can dream up (Baseball theme? Astronaut theme? Equestrian theme?).

3. Choose a foreign country and prepare an ethnic meal at home. On separate pieces of paper write the words *language, dress, geography, industry, history, government,* and *artists.* Each person picks a slip of paper from a hat and must prepare one minute's worth of information about the subject written on the paper. Go to the library as a family and spend thirty minutes finding the information. Return home, and let each person make a presentation while you eat your ethnic meal.

Recreation

1. Go camping. If you can't go away, set up a tent in your backyard. Pretend you are in the mountains. Roast hot dogs and marshmallows. Sing camp songs.

2. Take road trips. Pack up the car and explore a new section of the city or countryside on a Saturday. Before you begin, use a map and, as a family, decide on a new territory to cover. For a learning activity, give your child a pad of paper and pencil to record his thoughts about what he sees. Encourage him to go beyond simply describing the new place, and have

him jot notes of his impressions—how it makes him feel, what he finds interesting, what he likes and does not like about it. He could even start a "Road Trip Diary." At the end of the day, tell each other what you enjoyed about the trip.

3. Attend a sports event together. A fun follow-up activity would be to create a family sports page that records the event. Take a camera to the game and photograph the action, the crowd, and your family. Bring home a game program to refer to as you create your sports page. You can create the normal sports headlines and have fun creating headlines about your family: "Crowd Honored by Special Visit from the Johnson Family," or "Johnsons Set Record in Hot Dog Eating." Paste your photographs on the page, write or type the stories, and list the scores and statistics.

Together Emotionally

Creating intimacy as a family involves sharing feelings. Ironically, this can be most difficult with the very people with which you spend the most time. It is important to maintain a balance between holding all your feelings inside you and sharing every emotion that you have. On one hand, constantly telling someone how you feel can be draining on the other person. On the other hand, keeping your feelings bottled up can be draining on you.

Feelings Grab Bag

On slips of paper write terms that describe different emotions. Write one emotion on each piece of paper. Place the pieces of paper in a bag, and ask one person to choose a term from the bag. That person tells the family of a recent time when she felt that emotion and why. It can be something that occurred outside or inside the family. If your family is not used to talking about feelings, it may be good to start by talking about events outside the family that triggered a certain feeling. Later, as you feel more at ease with intimacy, you can share feelings between family members that need to be discussed.

You can encourage conversation around the table by requiring that each person ask a question or make a comment about what the first person said.

On the slips of paper you can include feelings such as: frustrated, angry, happy, giggly, afraid, lonely, hurt, relieved, proud, sad, regretful, loving, peaceful, excited, tired, worried, disappointed, embarrassed, compassionate, cheerful, and pleased.

Compliment Concert

The object of this activity is to learn to give and receive compliments and to build someone up with kind words. Choose a family member and have everyone else say one nice thing about that person.

Make Family Conversation a Game

Write open-ended questions on slips of paper, and place them in a jar. Each person takes turns selecting a question and answering it. The other family members can practice their conversational skills by asking follow-up questions, making comments, or relating similar experiences as the one told by the person who selected the original question. (See chapter 7 for details on conversational skills.)

Open-ended questions that work well are:

- What was something that happened to you today that you liked?
- What frustrated you today?
- Tell us about someone you talked to today and what you talked about.
- Who is a good friend of yours, and why do you like this person?

Other Resources for Creating Family Togetherness

An excellent book on establishing family traditions is *Let's Make a Memory* by Gloria Gaither and Shirley Dobson, published by Word in 1983. It provides fun ideas on how to turn each holiday into a time filled with special remembrances.

For dozens of projects designed to cultivate learning skills in your children, refer to Dorothy Rich's *MegaSkills,* published by Houghton Mifflin in 1988. It divides activities into age levels and ties them to the development of major academic skills.

Summary

Being together as a family both physically and emotionally creates an important foundation for academic success. By loving and accepting your children, you make your home a safe place for them to take risks in applying themselves to new learning tasks. Their fear of failure will decrease when they know that they will not lose your respect and love if they fall short. In this environment there is no emotional penalty for failure if they truly try. Your example will play an important role in establishing your children's priorities in life. They will look to you for what is important. Your family will take on its own sense of identity based on what you emphasize through traditions and the telling of family stories. The quantity and quality of your family's time together will be the rope that helps your children climb the obstacles of life.

In the next chapter we will look at another strong rope for helping your child succeed in school: academic goal setting.

12
Teach Goal Setting

Parent Power Tool #10:
Establish Goals as a Family

Your Goal
We have several clearly defined and written goals and are actively progressing toward their accomplishment. We encourage goal setting with each child.

I hate the subject of this chapter. Goal setting is a challenging subject for me. Goals hold me accountable. They are an objective measurement of success and failure. They make me feel guilty when I do frivolous things. Maybe you feel the same way. The fact that I hate them is all the more reason why I need them.

Goal setting and goal accomplishment are essential for your child's academic learning. Certainly, he can learn things about a subject without setting out to do so. We all pick up incidental knowledge about things just by living. But his real learning comes through fixing his eyes on a goal and exerting consistent effort toward reaching it.

Goals help us live with purpose. Without written goals, I tend to move from task to task as my desires dictate. My priorities are set by my moods. Often I find that I stay focused on one task too long. If I have a series of goals written down and divided into daily or weekly parts, I am able to juggle multiple tasks better. Without them, I tend to stick with the tasks I like best until I get interrupted by some unforeseen immediacy, which leads me entirely off course.

Goal setting and goal accomplishment are skills like learning to type or learning to ride a bicycle. They take discipline and practice, and after many frustrating attempts, you learn how to do it and it becomes second nature. It becomes a habit. I am still working on making it a habit, but I know what it is that successful goal setters do, and I will share their secrets with you.

The definition of the word *goal* is simple: an objective toward which an endeavor is directed. That definition has three components that are worthy of closer scrutiny: objective, endeavor, and directed. Without each of those components, goal achievement is impossible.

Establishing an Objective

Your child's first task is to outline his objective. What does he want to accomplish? This may seem so obvious that it is not worth mentioning, but having a clearly defined objective is not only crucial, it is also rare for most students. They might have a general notion in their heads of what they want to accomplish. Many students may have a goal to receive a particular grade for a class. Contrary to what you may think—though it may be a worthy goal to get an A from an English class—this is not a specific enough goal. The grade your child receives in a class is symbolic of what he has learned. Although it is good to have an overall objective of high marks in class, it is better to have a goal of mastering the set of skills and knowledge necessary to receive those high marks. Do you see the difference? To strive for an A in history is very different from striving to understand and master the knowledge of history and the skills involved in analyzing and evaluating history.

Let me give an example from an English class. Suppose your son is starting a new year in Mrs. Smith's English class. You want your son to learn valuable communication skills as well as get good grades.

To do that, you can have a conference with your child and the teacher to review what will be expected of your child during the course. Ask the teacher specifically what your child will be learning and what skills he will need to demonstrate in order to be rewarded with high grades. Before the conference, call the teacher or send her a letter similar to the following:

Dear Mrs. Smith,
    We are really happy that Roger will be in your English class this semester. We've heard wonderful things about

you. We want to reinforce at home what you will be teaching, and it would help me tremendously if we could schedule a conference to discuss two items: (1) what specific content you will be teaching in the next unit, and (2) what skills Roger will be learning in that unit. Would it be possible for me to receive an outline at our conference of the content and skills that Roger will need to demonstrate in order to do well in your class? Please call me to arrange a time to meet. Thanks for taking the time to do this.

The list the teacher gives you will be the basis for your child's goal setting for that class. It will also give you a guideline for monitoring his goal accomplishment. Rather than having a vague goal of "getting an A on my essay," he can have a specific goal of "understanding and demonstrating mastery in writing using the three parts of a persuasive essay." This concrete goal provides a clear line of action for your child to follow and for you to monitor.

Knowledge and Skills

When you confer with the teacher, ask her to provide you with specific content your child will need to learn and particular skills he will learn and demonstrate. Russ, a seventh-grade math, science, and English teacher, told me, "In my 22 years of teaching, I have yet to hear of a teacher who gets upset because a parent is involved in supporting a child's learning." To give you a better idea of what you are looking for, here are a few samples. They are not in order according to any particular grade level.

Knowledge

- Vocabulary words
- Multiplication tables
- The history of Lincoln's presidency
- The War of 1812

- Parts of speech in a sentence
- The rules of basketball

Skills

- Phonetic spelling
- Multiplying two- and three-digit numbers
- Analysis and chronological ordering of information
- Comparison of the War of 1812 with the Persian Gulf War
- Writing complete sentences
- Dribbling a basketball

Once you know what your child is supposed to learn, you can help him set appropriate goals. He will have concrete objectives to move toward.

The more specific information you can get from the teacher regarding knowledge and skills to be learned, the better for your child. Asking the teacher at the beginning of the semester to give you one list of all things she will teach in the next several months may be too much for you and her to process successfully. Dividing it into teaching units will be easier. Teachers tend to think in terms of units rather than weeks or months. For instance, Russ teaches a unit in his English class on plot and character development by having his students read an Agatha Christie mystery. While the students read the book, he wants them to discover what goes into a mystery and how it compares to other types of stories. If your child were in his class, you would ask him about the learning objectives of that particular unit.

Once your child has a clear idea of the objectives, he can set his goals. Any learning goal your child sets must have two components: (1) a measurable learning outcome and (2) a deadline. He must establish exactly what his goal accomplishment will look like. If it is not specific, he will not know when he has reached it. Examples of measurable learning outcomes are: "I will be able to multiply any two-digit numbers successfully" or "I will be able to name all the parts of a microscope and use it properly" or "I will be able to spell all the vocabulary words correctly."

Establishing a deadline helps your child focus his attention. He knows a day of accountability is coming. Adding deadlines to the goals above will make them complete: "I will be able to multiply any two-digit numbers successfully by the end of the week" or "I will be able to name the parts of a microscope and use it properly by tomorrow" or "I will be able to spell all the vocabulary words correctly before I go to bed." Remember, goal achievement will be easier and more meaningful for your child if:

1. He understands the learning objective.
   Example: "I will learn how to evaluate what distinguishes a mystery plot from other stories."
2. He sets a measurable learning goal.
   Example: "I will list the unique aspects of a mystery as I see them in Agatha Christie's *Murder on the Orient Express*."
3. He has a deadline for the goal.
   Example: "I will finish this by May 12."

Goals from Roles

It may serve your child well to set his goals within the framework of his roles. Often we categorize goals under abstract headings, such as English, science, math, homework, sports, and hobbies. That can work fine, but it doesn't explicitly address the issue of responsiblity. They are goals without goal achievers. They can stand on their own as if the person pursuing the goal doesn't matter.

A more effective way to approach setting a goal is by fully embracing the responsibility for its success. Your child can do this by setting his goals in keeping with the many roles he fills. Instead of saying, "What do I need to do in English class?" he asks, "What do I need to do in my role as an English student?" "In English class" is more impersonal than "as an English student." The distinction may, at first, appear to be splitting hairs, but it has an effect on his attitude. As an English *student* he has a responsibility. He is on the inside, fully engulfed in the duty. If he is just "in English class," he is more of an observer; he is outside looking in. The difference is between who he is as a person and what class he merely attends.

The goals created out of roles look different from everyday goals that become lists of "to dos" or action steps. Roles help us think in terms of our larger progress. Based upon your child's role as an English student, his goal for the week may be to thoroughly understand the three-part essay. He will have several action steps to accomplish that goal (which are goals in their own right). When he thinks in terms of his role as an English student, he can think about the big picture. The questions he can ask (or you can ask him) are, "How am I doing *right now* as an English student?" "What *progress* am I making toward being a better English student?" The difference between action steps and goals-from-roles is like the difference between examining each brush stroke of a painting and standing back to enjoy the full canvas. If you have ever watched an artist in action, you have noticed that he moves back and forth between applying paint and standing back to view his efforts in relation to the whole. Goals born out of roles will help your child gain the right perspective and assume more responsibility for his learning.

To help your child clearly define her role, you can create a list. At the top of a piece of paper write, for example, "The Responsiblities I Have in My Role as a Math Student." Discuss with your child the behavioral responsibilities she has in her role as a math student. If she comes up with the ideas on her own, she will take greater ownership of the responsibility. For example, she may say "I will pay attention in class," "I will treat the teacher with respect," "I will turn in all my assignments on time, and they will be done to the best of my ability." After you have discussed and listed those things, list more specific objectives from the role of math student. To do this you will need to refer to the information about knowledge and skills the teacher gave you. List the objectives your child will meet for the unit she is studying in the class. Periodically refer to the list you created and discuss with your child how she is doing in her role as math student.

Endeavor

A goal is not worth much if you don't apply effort to achieve it. Without effort toward its accomplishment a goal is only a dream. Someone once said if a man wants his dreams to come true, he must wake up. Many students fail to achieve their academic goals because they lack the will to make a consistent effort toward achieving them.

Effort to achieve requires dogged determination and discipline—something we all lack to one degree or another. A millionaire once gave me a bit of his guiding wisdom on how to be a successful goal achiever. He observed that successful people make a habit of doing the things that failures don't like to do. Goal achievers stick with the job until it is done. Goal achievers push just a little bit more, reach just a little bit higher, and concentrate just a little bit harder than those people who fail to reach their goals.

Discipline to Endeavor

What do you do if your child is not putting forth the effort to achieve his goals? You must help him find internal discipline. Discipline is something that grows from the outside in. It is imposed upon us until we make it a habit. Here are some suggestions for helping your child learn to develop self-discipline:

Limits. Set up clear and consistently enforced limits for your child. Limits create for a child what education specialist Lawrence Greene calls a natural sense of order and stability.[1] Rules for housework, homework, bedtime, and television viewing help a child understand and internalize the kind of self-control necessary for goal achievement. Rules create stability for a child. He sees that life is lived with a sense of order. Lack of limits fosters an undisciplined child who lacks the skills of self-discipline. He is not disciplined because he has seldom been called on to be disciplined, nor has he seen it modeled in his home.

Standards. Set up reasonable, yet challenging, standards for performance on homework assignments. Take into account the relative ability of your child. For instance, a young child with poor fine-motor skills will have difficulty writing neatly. However, if you have seen him write neatly in the past, it is reasonable to hold him responsible for consistently repeating that level of performance.

As you hold him to performance standards, you are giving him an important confidence boost. You are signaling to him that you recognize in him the ability to achieve. As he achieves at those higher levels, his sense of pride and self-satisfaction will propel him to greater discipline.

Rewards. Use appropriate rewards. Some people fear that rewarding a student for achieving a goal is a form of bribery. They fear that it will adulterate what should be purely a love for learning. However, experience has shown that children can move beyond meeting the performance standard for the sake of the reward and will continue the new levels of performance on their own. This occurs for two reasons: (1) their newfound internal discipline becomes a habit, and (2) they realize that they can achieve higher levels and enjoy the feeling of such accomplishment.

The child is eventually motivated by internal rewards, such as the good feeling from accomplishing the goal or maintaining something within his responsibility. The parent guides the child but allows him greater self-regulation toward fulfilling his responsibility.

Plugging Away

Your child's consistent efforts to achieve his objectives will lead him to success. He may not master a particular piece of content or a necessary academic skill at his first attempt. However, if he sticks with it and masters it, he will move ahead in doing well in class. Too many students rush through a lesson without really learning it. They are fixated on finishing the homework, not learning the content. In the end, their accumulation of muddled learning will bog them down. They will trudge through their education like a person trying to walk in ankle-deep mud. But if your child sticks with it and masters each skill or lesson the teacher relates to him, he will walk on the dry ground of educational confidence.

Directed

I remember being at Disneyland with my family, and we all decided to go on a particular ride. As we approached its entrance, we noticed a line that must have had one hundred people in it waiting to get on the ride. We looked to the front of the line and noticed the park attendant vainly attempting to wave people over to another entrance, which had no line at all. Failing to see the point of standing behind one hundred other people, we followed the attendant's direction and immediately got onto the ride. As we pulled away from the loading dock we looked back and, to our amazement, saw that no one had moved from his position. No one dared risk losing his place in line! They had forgotten their original objective of getting on the ride and had unconsciously changed their objective to dutifully standing in line.

Remember the definition of a goal: an objective toward which an endeavor is *directed*. After setting an objective and committing the energy to achieving it, it is imperative for your child to stay focused—keeping his efforts directed toward the objective. Lack of focus is most likely the number-one enemy of achieving goals. The problem of focus stems from four areas: priorities, distinctions, distractions, and desires.

Priorities

Setting priorities will help your child stay focused. It involves writing down, in order of importance, what objectives he should pursue. It also means determining the time he will spend on each objective. He may need to finish his book report, which is due in three days, but that does not mean he works exclusively on his book report at the expense of his other responsibilities.

A specific objective's priority is determined by its deadline, the results your child will gain from its completion or the negative consequences from not completing it, and its importance in relationship to your child's other responsibilities. When you work with your child to help him set his priorities for school, home, and recreation, have him ask himself these questions:

1. When do I need to complete this goal?
2. What will be the result of successfully meeting this goal?
3. How important is this goal in relation to the other things I need to do?

Distinctions

A well-defined goal provides distinction. It differentiates itself from other tasks. The distinction will help him focus on what is important. For instance, the teacher may assign him to "read the chapter on industrialism in the 1800s." The problem is that the assignment is vague and the learning objective is absent. There are too many things to absorb in the chapter, and it is unclear where your child's focus should be. If that happens, help your child create his own learning objectives from the chapter. He should survey the chapter, taking note of its subtitles, pictures, graphs, and questions at the end. On a separate piece of paper he should write a few questions he can ask while reading the chapter. That will help him focus his attention.

For instance, the chapter he is to read is on industrialism in the 1800s. The only assignment the teacher gave him was to read pages 574 through 578. You can help him focus his learning by first having him scan the section. Its subheadings are "Chief characteristics," "New inventions," "The spread of industrialism," "Growth of world trade," "Business consolidates," and "Workers unite." The child can then write some questions related to each subhead, using the format of who, what, when, where, why, and how. For example:

Chief characteristics:

1. What were the chief characteristics of industrialism?
2. When did they appear?
3. Where did they appear?

New inventions:

1. What were the new inventions during this time?
2. Who invented them?
3. Where were they invented?
4. What did they do to help industry?

This method will help him focus his attention. It will also make the reading more meaningful and increase his efficiency in reading the assigned pages. Most important, it will deepen his understanding of the subject.

The teacher may provide greater distinction to her assignment by adding that the child should answer the questions at the end of the chapter. This is a more distinct goal, and it helps your child focus his attention on the portions of the chapter that will help him answer the questions.

A word of caution about reading only to answer textbook questions: It is not unusual for students to use a hunt-for-the-answer approach and not learn anything at all. Many students learn the trick of answering textbook chapter questions by locating the words or phrases in the text that are similar to those in the question. Then they write down what, at first glance, appears to be the answer. Even if they are correct, they haven't really digested the answer. Worse yet, if they are sloppy in using the legitimate technique of skimming for data, they may actually write down an entirely wrong answer. For instance, the question may be "What is the climate of the Kalahari Desert?" The sloppy student may skim the page until he sees the phrase, "The climate of the Kalahari Desert." His eyes stop there and, assuming that a description is to follow, copies the rest of the sentence, ". . . creates both abundance and famine." This becomes his answer, which, if he had read the text, he would see is entirely wrong. In his haste, he missed the fact that the textbook goes on to give a clear description of the climate, not just its result. Haste in completing the assignment is often the culprit in defocusing a student from the real objective of learning.

You can help your child make his goals even more distinctive by listing the knowledge as well as the skills he will learn or practice. Students perform better when they know what it is they are supposed to learn or demonstrate. For instance, using our example above, a very distinctive goal regarding the assignment would be to learn the weather patterns of Africa and how they affect its agriculture. He will demonstrate skill in using maps and charts as well as learn to find sufficient information to answer the question. Once he has gained clear focus by prioritizing and distinguishing what his goal is, he still runs the risk of not achieving his goal due to distractions.

Distractions

Whenever you say yes to one thing, you say no to something else. One way for your child to overcome distractions is for her to clearly acknowledge what she is saying no to when she says yes to her homework. In the process she will learn to delay her gratification and plan her time better.

Sit down with your child and, together, set up a schedule for when she will do her homework each day. During that time she knows she cannot play with her friends, watch TV, or work on a hobby (she may enjoy the fact that during this time she won't be asked to do household chores, either). Create a homework habit in your child by establishing a set time for your child to work on schoolwork. Even if she doesn't have enough homework to fill the allotted time, she can always review her work for a future test, read ahead, double-check her work, or read a good novel. Allowing her to vary the time she spends on her homework based on her daily work load may encourage her to give in to the distractions of other, more fun things. If she wants to go out to play in the neighborhood and reasons that her math assignment will take only fifteen minutes to complete if she hurries, she will be tempted to do less than her best. Instead, if she knows that she *must* spend one hour on her homework, she won't have the temptation to hurry through it. She will be able to better focus on her work.

Desires

Finally, your child's focus on homework is affected by his desires. If he is not internally motivated by desire, he may go through the motions but lack the proper enthusiasm to achieve well. Desire is absolutely crucial for achievement. Without the want to, there is no will to; without the will to, there is no way to achieve.

Your child's desires come from a variety of influences. His desires are shaped by what is important to you and to what you show approval. They are also shaped by what he has an aptitude for and the positive feedback he receives from others when he demonstrates that aptitude. If he shows talent for playing the piano and receives peoples' approval and encouragement, it is likely that he will want to continue developing this musical ability.

A child's desires for one thing can be influenced by desires for another thing. For example, he may want to excel in a particular sport because his friends participate in that sport, and he wants to be admired and appreciated by them. She may want to do well in a math class because she wants to get a higher overall grade-point average.

Desires can be developed from within (as from aptitudes) and developed externally (as through praise, encouragement, and rewards). You can help your child develop the desire for academic achievement by analyzing his aptitudes and those external things he desires. Then, tie academic accomplishment to those aptitudes and external motivators.

Take, for example, a hypothetical situation for Kirk and his mother, Joanne. After taking inventory of Kirk's aptitudes,

Joanne realizes—though he has a talent with numbers—that he consistently does sloppy work and is only receiving mediocre grades in math class. She also knows that he wants a new skateboard. Together they establish a learning goal which will earn him the new skateboard. She buys the skateboard and allows him to keep it in his room but stipulates that he cannot use it until he has reached the mutually established goal. Joanne also keeps the receipt for the purchase and lets Kirk know that the skateboard can be easily returned to the store if he fails to reach the goal. Finally, she clearly communicates that she is available to help him reach his goal by monitoring his work and offering encouragement. She has provided a powerful incentive for Kirk to refine his math skills. It won't be long before he no longer needs an external reward to do his best in math.

Think about your child. What desires has he expressed lately? Can those be directed toward helping him in his academic achievement?

Summary

Goal setting is a powerful tool for academic success. To use goals properly your child will need to clearly set objectives, put forth effort to reach those objectives, and stay focused on the tasks. It may help him take greater responsibility for his goals if he sees himself fulfilling a variety of roles. When you create a disciplined environment at home regarding homework, you are helping him learn to be disciplined. You are helping your child set priorities and keeping him away from distractions. Tangible rewards can be powerful motivators to keep him directed toward accomplishing his goals. In time, he will grow out of the need for the external incentive and will be internally motivated by his own sense of achievement. In the end, after you have done all you can do to create a positive public school experience for your child, it will be up to him to develop the internal desire and discipline to achieve, and goal setting can help him do this.

A Final Word
on Creating a Positive Public
School Experience

I began this book by stating that we all know public schools need reform. If you have been involved with your school you have most likely noticed that changes are occurring. It seems that every school in the country is implementing some new method in an attempt to help children learn better. Some schools will succeed, and others will fail to achieve any better results. The only way you can ensure that your child will do well in school is to take personal responsibility for his or her academic development. That's what this book is all about.

When you build a positive relationship with your child's teachers you will be doing more than just helping your child. You will be touching the life of each teacher as well. Often Christians focus exclusively on the plight of the children in the public school setting without regard for the plight of the teachers there. As much as anyone else, they need to see good examples of caring Christian parents who nurture their children. Teachers not only have their classroom children to oversee, but they are often parents themselves. Your example can be a powerful influence on their personal lives.

At Gateways To Better Education, we emphasize relational activism—building relationships with teachers as well as with your child—because lives are changed through relationships. Imagine if out of all the students a teacher has, ten of them have Christian parents who reach out to and work with the teacher in the ways described here. Imagine if out of six hundred students in a school, one hundred Christian parents were actively and positively involved in the school. The influence on the administration and teachers could be revolutionary!

In Matthew 9:37–38, Jesus tells his disciples, "The harvest is plentiful, but the workers are few. Therefore beseech the Lord of the harvest to send out workers into His harvest." Note that Matthew prefaced Jesus' admonition to evangelize with an observation about Jesus that is instructive for us. In 9:36 he writes, "And seeing the multitudes, He felt compassion for them, because they were distressed and downcast like sheep without a shepherd." As Jesus saw people weary of the burdens of life and without direction, He did not respond in anger; He responded with compassion. He desired to do something about their plight.

It is easy to get angry about misguided programs in public schools. The more difficult response—but the response Jesus modeled for us—is one of compassion for a lost world. So remember, as you get involved with your child's public education, that your example and your relationship with school personnel may open up possibilities for you or someone else in the future to introduce the "sheep having no shepherd" to the Good Shepherd Himself. And then, for that teacher, you will truly have created a positive public school experience!

Appendix
Your Thirty-Day Program for Maximum Success

You may feel overwhelmed after reading all the previous chapters. We have covered so much material that it would be nearly impossible to implement it all at once. That is why I have included a thirty-day program for you to follow. It includes many of the main ideas contained in the book. Follow it each day, and you will see tremendous improvement in your child's achievement. Each daily program is designed for the busy parent, and most of the activities take only a few minutes.

You can use this dynamic program throughout the school year. Each daily activity includes special instructions so you can repeat it after the first thirty-day period. These instructions are listed under the Extended Success Program at the end of each day. The second time around you will be improving your performance, modifying something, or monitoring something you started the first time. In this way the thirty-day program can become a sixty-day, ninety-day, and even a 180-day program!

Fast-Track Program

If you want to focus immediately on some specific areas, you can arrange the activities according to a customized Fast-Track Program. With this program you do not have to wait to implement an activity until the programmed day. It groups related activities together so you can pay special attention to one area of need. Here is how to use the Fast-Track Program:

Step 1: Refer to the scores you gave yourself for each of the ten Parent Power Tools in chapter 2. Transfer those scores into the spaces provided below.

Step 2: Based on your scores, decide which Power Tool you need to work on.

Step 3: Refer to the days listed to the right of the Parent Power Tools scoring box. These are the days that have activities designed to help you strengthen that Power Tool.

Parent-teacher relations	_____	Day 1, 11, 21
Understand the culture	_____	Day 2, 12, 22
Encouragement in home	_____	Day 3, 13, 23
Show interest in subject	_____	Day 4, 14, 24
Maximize reading	_____	Day 5, 15, 25
Limit television	_____	Day 6, 16, 26
Conversation that promotes thinking	_____	Day 7, 17, 27
Spiritual emphasis	_____	Day 8, 18, 28
Family togetherness	_____	Day 9, 19, 29
Goal setting	_____	Day 10, 20, 30

The Thirty-Day Implementation Program

Day 1: Parent-Teacher Relationship Building

Write an affirming note to your child's teacher(s), giving a specific example of something you appreciate about his/her teaching. To get your creativity flowing, brainstorm on several specific things you could write about. They do not have to be profound learning break-throughs your child demonstrated; they can be the simple, often overlooked things. Refer to chapter 3 if you need help.

A good thing you have observed in your child or the teacher:

_____

_____

_____

Write the letter using the best ideas you thought of.
Mail the letter to the teacher. The school's address is:

_____

_____

For the Extended Success Program: Make a habit of reviewing your child's classroom experience and letting the teacher know how he or she positively influenced your child.

Day 2: Family Code of Honor

On a separate piece of paper, write your family's code of honor. That includes statements of what you want your family to believe about certain values, attitudes, and character qualities. Refer to the section in chapter 4 entitled "Tour Guide Training."

1. Once you have clearly defined honor statements, use them to discuss values with your children.
2. Write the value statements on six-by-nine-inch cards and post one each week on your refrigerator. That becomes your Word for the Week and the focus of your values instruction and discussion.
3. Talk about the Word for the Week during mealtimes or other family gatherings. Explain what it means and why it is important. Ask each family member to give an example of how it can be beneficial. You could even have your family develop a skit to role model the good quality.

Family Honor Code Topics			
Respect	Responsibility	Honesty	Punctuality
Self-control	Kindness	Courage	Helpfulness
Cleanliness	Thrift	Self-reliance	Courtesy
Patience	Sportsmanship	Loyalty	Citizenship
Cheerfulness	Generosity		

For the Extended Success Program: Going through the words listed above will take eighteen weeks. Continue the practice with other values you think of, or recycle these for emphasis.

Day 3: Encouraging Good Character

List three things your child did in the last week that pleased you. Match that behavior with good character qualities you want to encourage. Look for opportunities to encourage your child by recognizing his behavior and revealing his good qualities. Refer to chapter 5 for more help.

Example: Behavior—he did a thorough job helping me wash the car. Quality—he demonstrated the character quality of thoroughness by noticing details. (For ideas, see the list of qualities on pages 77–78.)

Three behaviors I recognized:

1. _____

2. _____

3. _____

The character qualities the behaviors revealed:

1. _____

2. _____

3. _____

Discuss your findings with your child.

For the Extended Success Program: Repeat this exercise as often as you like.

Day 4: Knowing Your Child's Academic Subject

Ask your child what subject she is learning in school that she finds most interesting. (You may already know the answer.) Get a book from the library on that subject and begin reading about it. (You may not have to read the entire book. Instead, just read the chapter or section that deals with the subject your child is learning. See chapter 6 under "Read About the Subject" for more help.)

The subject my child finds most interesting right now is:

_____

The book I found in the library to read about that subject:

_____

List the three things you found most interesting about that subject:

1. _____

2. _____

3. _____

Discuss your findings with your child.

For the Extended Success Program: During the next thirty-day program cycle, choose a book on the subject your child finds least interesting. You might also try to find a videotape on the subject or look for a television program that covers that topic.

Day 5: Learning to Use Your Library

Take your entire family to the local public library. Allow at least one hour. Arrange ahead of time for the librarian to give you a guided tour. Have him/her explain each of the many information sources the library contains and how to use them. Conclude your activity by having each family member check out a book. Refer to the section entitled "How to Maximize Reading Skills" in chapter 7.

Local library telephone number:

_____

The hours your library is open:

_____

Librarian who will conduct the tour:

_____

Date and time your family will go:

_____

For the Extended Success Program: 1. During the next thirty-day cycle, set up a library scavenger hunt. 2. Go to the library, as a family, at least once each month.

Day 6: Limiting Television Viewing

Estimate the amount of television your family watches each week, and write that amount in the space provided below. Get a television guide and, as a family, mark the shows you want to watch. Start today trying to cut your viewing time in half. For example, if you normally watch thirty hours of TV each week, try to cut it to fifteen hours this week. (Of course, if you watch less than thirty minutes each day or do not have a television set, this activity is not for you.)

Family Member   Time Spent Watching TV

_____   _____

_____   _____

_____   _____
_____   _____
_____   _____
_____   _____
Total hours: _____   _____

Cutting the normal amount of viewing time in half will result in watching no more than _____ hours of television this week.

List three activities you can suggest that your child (or spouse) do instead of watching television:

1. _____
2. _____
3. _____

For the Extended Success Program: Continue to reduce the amount of time your children watch television until they have broken the viewing habit.

Day 7: Conversation with Your Child

Make a special effort today to have extended dialogue with your child. For help, refer to the section in chapter 6 entitled "Talk About the Subject" and refer to chapter 9. To get started, use the space below to write down some key topics to discuss.

1. _____
2. _____
3. _____

For the Extended Success Program: Make a conscious effort to listen to your child's ideas while making only empathetic remarks that encourage him to keep talking. Purposely restrain yourself from giving in to the urge to make a suggestion or a correction unless he asks for it (or unless what he is talking about doing is something that will seriously harm him).

Day 8: Spiritual Growth

Today, reflect on your child's well-being in things other than physical or material comforts. Circle T or F to indicate if the sentences below are true or false about your child's development. If you have more than one child, write each child's name after the appropriate sentence.

T/F 1. My child is more materialistic than I would like him/her to be.

T/F 2. My child seems to think of God in a personal way, not as an abstract deity.

T/F 3. My child does not seem to care about other people.

T/F 4. My child struggles when deciding what is right and wrong.

T/F 5. My child seldom (or never) seems to think about God.

T/F 6. I do not encourage my child to investigate religious truths.

T/F 7. We attend religious services regularly as a family.

T/F 8. I regularly pray for my child's mental, physical, spiritual, and emotional needs.

T/F 9. I regularly talk to my child about how God is working in my life.

T/F 10. In the past several months, I have definitely seen an improvement in my child's knowledge and application of God's Word.

Write down any concerns these ten statements have prompted with regard to your family's spiritual development.

_____

_____

_____

_____

Now, write at least one thing you will do to begin improving in each area of concern.

For the Extended Success Program: In thirty days, go through the ten statements again, and see if any of your answers have changed. If so, celebrate! If not, try a different strategy for improvement.

Day 9: Family Folklore

Pour yourself a cup of coffee, and spend a little time reminiscing. To enrich your family's oral history, create six headlines that herald stories you have not yet told your children about your past or your family's history. The stories can be funny, adventurous, heartwarming, sad, or interesting. Tell at least one of these stories to your family today.

Headlines
1. _____
2. _____
3. _____
4. _____
5. _____
6. _____

For the Extended Success Program: In the next thirty-day cycle, repeat this exercise with six new stories.

Day 10: Setting Expectations

Take a few minutes today to establish homework expectations for your child. As you answer each question, keep in mind that your expectations should be challenging yet reasonable. It is a good idea to get the child's input when setting your standards. For help, refer to chapter 6 under the subheading "Make Learning a Priority in Your Home" and chapter 12 under "Endeavor."

1. The biggest distraction for my child while doing homework is:_____.
2. Ideas for eliminating that distraction:_____
   _____.
3. The time to do homework will be from when to when each day?_____
4. The place to do homework will be (what room of the house)?_____
5. List the things you think your child needs to improve the most when doing homework.

   _____

   _____

   _____

6. What will be your standards for quality on the things you listed above? (In other words, how will you know when your child meets your expectations?)

_____

_____

_____

7. Have you provided all the resources your child needs to do a good job? If not, what else could you provide (both physically and emotionally)?

_____

_____

8. What will be your child's reward when he/she meets your expectations? _____ (physically or emotionally)

For the Extended Success Program: Review the eight questions and look for improvement or make adjustments as needed.

Day 11: Scheduling a Parent-Teacher Conference

Call the school today, and leave a message for the teacher requesting a conference. When you schedule the conference, be sure to request a list of the teacher's objectives for student knowledge and skills. (See chapter 12 under "Objectives." For more help, refer to chapter 3 under "Having Terrific Parent-Teacher Conferences"; chapter 4 under "Public School Cultural Factors," and chapter 7 under "How to Maximize Reading Skills.")

Complete the following tasks on a separate piece of paper.

1. Write down the date, time, and place of the conference along with the teacher's name.
2. List everyone who will be at the meeting.
3. List the specific questions you want answered about your child.
4. Write down two positive things about your child that you will tell the teacher.
5. Write down two positive things about the teacher or school you can convey to her at the conference.
6. List any instructional methods or subjects that you do not understand and need explained.
7. Ask if your child is performing to grade level according to state standards.
8. Ask for an extra copy of the textbook or material.

9. Ask for the teacher's specific objectives for what your child will know (content) and be able to do (skills) during the next unit.
10. Near the end of the meeting, ask:

- What are the next goals for my child?
- How can I monitor his progress?
- What can I do to support you and my child in reaching those goals?

For the Extended Success Program: Go through the same questions each time you have a conference. Keep your notes so you can evaluate your child's progress accurately.

Day 12: Getting to Know Your School Better

Provide answers for the instructions below. Then choose one thing to do within the next thirty days.

1. List one event you can attend at school within the next thirty days (your child may know of one if you don't).

   _____

2. List three ways you can volunteer at school. It could be a one-time visit or an ongoing involvement. Refer to chapter 3 under "Step Two: Lend a Hand" for ideas.

   _____

   _____

   _____

3. Call the school district administration offices and find out when your school board meets next.
   Date and Time:_____
   Plan to attend.

For the Extended Success Program: Repeat this exercise during the next thirty-day cycle, and choose a way to get involved with your school on a regular or occasional basis.

Day 13: Encouraging Skill Development

Just as you did on Day 3, list three things your child did that pleased you recently. This time, match those behaviors with good skills you want to encourage. Finally, look for opportunities to encourage your child by recognizing his behavior and revealing his good abilities. Refer to chapter 5 for more help. Example: Behavior—she neatly colored her map of the United States. Skill—she demonstrated neatness. (For ideas, see the list on page 82.)

Three behaviors to recognize:
1. _____
2. _____
3. _____

The skills the behaviors reveal:
1. _____
2. _____
3. _____

For the Extended Success Program: Repeat this exercise as often as you like

Day 14: Review Your Child's Homework

Set up a systematic way to check the quality of your child's homework. Use this each day as you review his work. If you need help, refer to chapter 6 under "Make Learning a Priority in Your Home."

Use the following three quality controls to review your child's homework each night:

1. Yes or No—Is the homework done completely?
2. Yes or No—Is the homework done neatly?
3. Yes or No—Is the homework done on time?

If your answer is no to any of these questions, review chapter 6.

For the Extended Success Program: Make this exercise a habit when reviewing your child's homework.

Day 15: Monitoring Your Child's Reading Comprehension

To check your child's reading comprehension today, have him write a summary of whatever homework reading assignment he has.

Have him answer the questions listed below under Section A. When you evaluate his answers, ask yourself the questions listed under Section B. *Keep in mind your child's grade-level ability.* For help on this, refer to chapter 7 under "How to Maximize Reading Skills."

Section A (for student)
1. List any words in your reading that you did not understand.
2. Summarize the story (if there is a story) or the main idea (if the passage was informational) in one paragraph.
3. What did you like or dislike about what you read?
4. (If your child reads a story) What do you think the author's overall message was in the story?

Section B (for evaluating student's comprehension)
1. Talk to the child's teacher about the vocabulary words your child indicated were new to him. Ask the teacher if your child should know these words at his grade level.
2. Was he able to summarize the story accurately and grasp the main idea?
3. Did he get distracted by unimportant details in his summary?
4. Did he focus on the wrong part of the story or passage?
5. On a scale of 1 to 10, rate his ability to express a personal reaction to the reading (this corresponds to Section A, question 3).
6. Was he able to grasp the author's underlying message conveyed by the story?

Compare his answers to the skills outlined in chapter 7. This will give you an informal idea of your child's reading comprehension level.

For the Extended Success Program: Repeat this activity at least once each quarter.

Day 16: Limiting Television Viewing

Write down which night your family watches the most television. Instead of watching all the TV programs that night, watch only one and videotape the rest. Watch the videotaped programs on a night when you don't watch as much TV. This activity will help you break free from scheduling activities around TV programing and allow you to try new activities.

The night we watch the most TV: _____

Shows we will videotape: _____
_____
_____
_____

List three *more* activities that you can suggest your child (or spouse) do instead of watching television:

1. _____
2. _____
3. _____

For the Extended Success Program: Try videotaping more programs and see if you like the freedom of seeing your favorite programs whenever you like.

Day 17: Conversational Skills

Teach your child the four key elements to a balanced conversation: shared experiences, comments, questions, and listening. For help with this, refer to chapter 9 under the subheading "Conversational Parts."

1. When will you teach these skills to your child?
   _____

2. Brainstorm with your child, and list at least ten general questions you can ask during a conversation that will enhance the dialogue. Some ideas to get you started: "Tell me more about that." "Why do you like that?"

3. Teach your child the four elements of Listening:

   H   HONOR the one speaking.
   E   Make EYE-CONTACT with the speaker.
   A   ASK yourself questions about what the speaker is saying.
   R   RESPOND to what the speaker says.

For the Extended Success Program: Evaluate how well your family practiced the four key elements of conversation this month (score your family from 1 to 10). Write down the element you feel your family needs to work on the most and work on improving it.

Day 18: The Spiritual Life

Focus on helping your child develop his understanding of God's promises, portraits, and protocol. Refer to chapter 10 to complete this activity.

God's Portraits
Pick one portrait (attribute) of God to highlight in family devotions this month. (If you don't have family devotions, begin having them using one of the following topics.)

Holy	Just	Righteous	Eternal	Unchanging
Wise	Omnipotent	Omniscient	Omnipresent	Good
Merciful	Gracious	Loving	Sovereign	Triune
Infinite				

God's Promises
Find one promise (per week) in the Bible that relates to the attribute you chose.

1. _____
2. _____
3. _____
4. _____

God's Protocol
Find four ways of living the Christian life (one per week) that relate to God's portrait or promises.

1. _____
2. _____
3. _____
4. _____

For the Extended Success Program: Repeat this activity and choose a different portrait, set of promises, and protocol principles.

Day 19: Family Togetherness

Schedule a family activity to experience something in the arts. Go to an art museum or gallery, a play, an opera, or a concert. Look in your newspaper, visit your chamber of commerce or the city's tourist office for ideas on where to go. Refer to chapter 11 for help.

1. The activity we choose to do this month is:

   _____

   When: _____

   Where: _____

2. The pre-event question or activity will be:

   _____

   _____

3. The post-event question or activity will be:

   _____

   _____

For the Extended Success Program: Repeat the activity. This time involve history, science, technology, foods, or recreation.

Day 20: The Roles of Your Child

Now would be a good time to help your child define his many roles. This will help him set and meet his goals.

1. On a separate sheet of paper, help your child define each of his roles. Review chapter 12 for assistance.
2. Together, create a poster that lists his roles. Hang it in his room.
3. Be sure to explain to him the relationship of roles and goals. Roles provide the basis for determining what your goals will be.

For the Extended Success Program: Review this activity at *least* once each month.

Day 21: Give a Good Plug for Your Child

Send a positive message about your child to his teacher. Refer to chapter 3 for help.

1. Write down one thing your child did at home that is related to his academic development. Ideas: He read a good book, didn't watch any TV, spent extra time on his homework, or demonstrated a thinking skill.

---

2. Write a short note commenting on this to your child's teacher.
3. *Mail* the note to the teacher. Enclose a stamped, self-addressed envelope.
   Example:

Dear Mrs. Sanders,
   I just thought you would like to know about the progress I've seen in Susan's attitude about homework (I've been working with her on this). Last night she spent a full hour on her science project without complaining on her part or nagging on mine. She really is becoming more responsible. Is her attitude improving in class as well? It would help me to know how she's doing in this area. Thanks.

For the Extended Success Program: Repeat this activity each month.

Day 22: Understanding the Classroom Culture

Give special attention to learning something about a teaching method or a curriculum used by your child's teacher. (Refer to chapter 4 for more specific information.)

1. List the terms, methodologies, or curricula that you do not understand (i.e., whole language, higher-order thinking skills, self-esteem course, dialectical journaling).

---

2. Write the telephone numbers of the people listed below who could help you understand the above listed terms, methods, or curricula.

	Name	Phone
Teacher		
Principal		
Curriculum Director		

3. Go to the local library (university libraries are also good sources), and research a book that addresses the term, method, or curriculum in question.
4. On a separate paper, list the pros and cons of the term, method, or curriculum (you could even ask the teacher, principal, or curriculum director their opinions).

For the Extended Success Program: Repeat this activity with another term, method, or curriculum that affects your child.

Day 23: Encouraging Good Qualities

On days 3 and 13 you identified good bahavior done by your child and looked for qualities that behavior revealed. Today you can reverse that pattern. Think of three character qualities you want your child to demonstrate, then look for recent examples of when he exhibited those qualities.

Example: Quality — You want him to demonstrate more generosity.
Behavior — You remember noticing that he shares his sports equipment with his friend. Make a point of commenting on that to him.
(For a list of ideas, see pages 77–78.)

Three character qualities:
1. _____
2. _____
3. _____

Three deeds that recently demonstrated those qualities:
1. _____
2. _____
3. _____

For the Extended Success Program: Repeat this exercise as often as you like.

Day 24: Applying a Subject to Life

Help your child see how an academic subject applies to real-world situations. Refer to chapter 6 for ideas.

1. Choose a subject you want to highlight for your child that is of particular interest to him. _____
2. List ways we use that subject in everyday living.

   _____

   _____

   _____

   _____

3. List occupations that use that subject.

   _____

   _____

4. Write down a place you can go to locally that routinely uses that subject or a skill related to that subject.

   _____

5. Schedule a date and time to introduce your child to that occupation by visiting the office, factory, or laboratory.
   Date: _____ Time: _____
   Contact Person: _____
   Location: _____

For the Extended Success Program: Repeat this exercise with a different academic subject, and this time choose a subject that your child struggles with.

Day 25: Double-Entry Journals

Introduce your teenager to double-entry journaling. This activity will help him develop his reading and thinking skills. Draw a line down the middle of a piece of paper. At the top of the left column, write "Quote." At the top of the right column write "My Thoughts." As your child reads a story (or his textbook) have him copy into the left column any words, phrases, or sentences he finds interesting. In the right column, next to the quote, ask him to write his thoughts about the quote. That teaches him to think while he is reading.

It may help to read the passage once and then review it to complete the journal. That way he won't interrupt the flow of his reading.

Quote (From Mark Twain's *Luck*)	My Thoughts
It was food and drink to me to look, and look, and look at that demigod....	Good description of being star- struck.
I could just barely have stood it if they had made him a cornet.	Cornet: what's that?
Here was a woodenhead whom I had put in the way of promotions.	Could he just be jealous of the other guy?

For the Extended Success Program: Have your child make this activity a regular part of his reading.

Day 26: Limiting Television Viewing

Estimate how well your family has done in limiting the amount of television you watch each week.

1. On a scale of 1–10, how much have you changed your TV habits since you read this book? (1=no change, 10=changed a lot) _____
2. Do you turn off the TV after watching a program and before the commercials start? _____
3. Do you mute the sound during commercials and talk about the story, plot, characters, or themes of the show? _____
4. Do your children select which shows they will watch from the TV guide at the beginning of the week? _____
5. Have you videotaped any shows and created your own TV schedule? _____

If you scored below a 5 on question 1 or answered no to questions 2–5, select one thing you will do tonight to take more control of your television viewing habits.

For the Extended Success Program:

Day 27: Talking About Thinking

Your child can learn better when he thinks about the various types of thinking (analysis, synthesis, comparison, relevance, etc.). Today's exercise will help you look for opportunities to teach a thinking skill to your child. See chapter 9 for help.

1. Review chapter 9 under the section entitled "Conversations About Thinking Skills."
2. Look at a homework assignment your child is working on today, and ask him to explain what he is supposed to do.
3. Choose a thinking skill your child must use in order to complete his homework, and explain the skill to him. Below are listed a variety of thinking skills.

Comparison	Contrast
Synthesis	Evaluation
Fact vs. opinion	Application
Problem-solving	Summarize
Cause and effect	Discerning bias
Following directions	Relevance
Classify	Categorize

For the Extended Success Program: Repeat this activity as often as you like.

Day 28: The Spiritual Life

Write a list of things you can pray about concerning your child's education. Refer to this list frequently.
Some ideas:

1. Your child's teacher(s).
2. Your child's friends.
3. The school principal and administration; the district superintendent; the school board.
4. Your child's moral, academic, and spiritual development.

Prayer topics:

1. _____
2. _____
3. _____

4. _____

5. _____

6. _____

7. _____

8. _____

9. _____

10._____

For the Extended Success Program: Repeat this activity with a new set of prayer requests.

Day 29: Being Together Emotionally

On slips of paper, write terms that describe different emotions. Write one emotion on each piece of paper. Place the pieces into a paper bag. Shake the bag and have each person choose a piece of paper. Then each person should tell of a recent incident that triggered the emotion written on his or her paper. The story can be about something that occurred outside the family. It could be something seen on TV or that happened at school, play, or work. Refer to chapter 11 under "Together Emotionally" for help.

Suggested emotions:

Frustrated	Angry	Peaceful	Cheerful
Happy	Giggly	Excited	Pleased
Afraid	Lonely	Tired	Laughter
Hurt	Relieved	Worried	Satisfied
Proud	Sad	Disappointed	Regretful
Appreciative	Loving	Embarrassed	Joyous

Tip: It may happen that the family member will describe an inappropriate emotional reaction to a situation. If that occurs, try to understand the person's perspective—why the event triggered that emotion—before attempting to gently guide him to a healthier or more mature response.

For the Extended Success Program: Repeat this activity as often as you like.

Day 30: Roles and Goals

If you have not already done so, today, work with your child in establishing his academic goals. If you have already done this, now would be a good time to review them. Refer to chapter 12 for help.

1. Review your child's roles and, together, determine his objectives. List them on a separate sheet of paper.
2. Ask him what resources he believes he needs in order to accomplish each objective. List them. If they are reasonable, provide them or help him get them.
3. Divide each objective into smaller daily or weekly goals. Set up a calendar and write each day's goal on the appropriate date.

For the Extended Success Program: Repeat this activity at least once each month.

Notes

CHAPTER THREE: Get Acquainted
1. Terry Frith, *Secrets Parents Should Know About Public Schools* (New York: Simon and Schuster, 1985), 67.
2. Ibid., 69.

CHAPTER FIVE: Build Character
1. Lawrence J. Greene, *Kids Who Underachieve* (New York: Simon and Schuster, 1986), 89.
2. Eric Buehrer, *Charting Your Family's Course* (Wheaton, IL: Victor Books, 1994), 108.
3. Dorothy Rich, *MegaSkills* (Boston: Houghton Mifflin, 1988), 19, 58, 83.
4. D. L. Silvernail, *Developing Positive Student Self-Concept* (Washington, D.C.: NEA Professional Library, 1985).
5. Susan Black, "Self-Esteem Sense and Nonsense," *The American School Board Journal*, July 1991, 27–29.
6. Ibid.
7. Ibid.
8. R. J. Calsyn and D. A. Kenny, "Self-Concept of Ability and Perceived Evaluation of Others: Cause or Effect of Academic Achievement?" *Journal of Educational Psychology*, 69 (1977), 136–45.

CHAPTER SIX: Boost Motivation
1. Samuel Blumenfeld, *How to Tutor* (New Rochelle, N.Y.: Arlington House, 1973), 144.

CHAPTER SEVEN: Maximize Reading
1. The five descriptions of reading proficiencies are taken directly from a United States government report written by Ina Mullis and Lynn Jenkins, *The Reading Report Card, 1978–88* (Washington, D.C.: The National Assessment of Educational Progress, January 1990), 23.
2. Terry Salinger, *Language Arts and Literacy for Young Children* (Columbus, Ohio: Merrill, 1988), 248.

3. (Need source for National Assessment of Educational Progress.)
4. Mary A. Foertsch, *Reading In and Out of School* (Washington, D.C.: National Center for Educational Statistics, May 1992), 36.

CHAPTER EIGHT: Limit Television

1. Brigtta Hoijer, "Television-Evoked Thoughts and Their Relation to Comprehension," *Communication Research* 16, 2 (April 1989), 179–203.
2. Jane Healy, *Endangered Minds* (New York: Simon & Schuster, 1990), 208–9.
3. Ibid., 219, 211.
4. James B. Twitchell, *Carnival Culture: The Trashing of Taste in America* (New York: Columbia University Press, 1992), 2.
5. Stephan Lesher, *Media Unbound* (Boston: Houghton Mifflin, 1982), 7.
6. Hoijer, "Television-Evoked Thoughts," 179–203.

CHAPTER NINE: Promote Thinking

1. Gordon Wells and Peter French, "Language in the Transition from Home to School" (Bristol, England: Center for the Study of Language and Communication, 1980). A report to the Nuffield Foundation.
2. Healy, *Endangered Minds,* 110.
3. Vincent Ruggiero, *Teaching Thinking Across the Curriculum* (New York: Harper and Row, 1988), 1.
4. Morry Van Ments, *Active Talk* (New York: St. Martin's Press, 1990), 86.

CHAPTER TEN: Dig Deeper

1. Quentin J. Schultze, et al., *Dancing in the Dark* (Grand Rapids: Eerdmans, 1991), 139.
2. Ibid., 8.
3. Ibid., 181.
4. Allan Bloom, *The Closing of the American Mind* (New York: Simon and Schuster, 1987), 25–26.

CHAPTER ELEVEN: *Create Togetherness*

1. Tom Peters and Nancy Austin, *A Passion for Excellence* (New York: Warner Books, 1985), 495–6.
2. Carlfred Broderick, *Understanding the Family Process* (Newbury Park, CA: Sage Publications, 1993), 198.
3. Ibid., 203.

CHAPTER TWELVE: *Teach Goal Setting*

1. Greene, *Kids Who Underachieve,* 223–5.

Index

About The Author

Eric Buehrer is president of Gateways To Better Education—a non-profit organization dedicated to helping families with children in public schools. He has spent the last nine years helping families with public school children. A former high school history teacher, Mr. Buehrer is in demand across the country as a speaker and counselor to parents and educators regarding public school issues. He has appeared on many national television and radio programs. When he's not playing with his daughter Katie, he enjoys snow skiing, family road trips, and a challenging game of chess with his wife, Kim. This is his third book.

For information on having Eric Buehrer
speak in your community write to:

Gateways To Better Education
P. O. Box 514
Lake Forest, CA 92630